GRAVES AND SITES
ON THE
OREGON AND
CALIFORNIA TRAILS

Randy Brown at work on the Millie Irwin fence with two of his students, Kassidy Falkenburg, age ten, and Gena Falkenburg, age eight. June 1998.

GRAVES AND SITES
ON THE
OREGON AND
CALIFORNIA TRAILS

Randy Brown
and
Reg Duffin

Oregon-California Trails Association
Independence, Missouri

Cover: Grave of Frederick Richard Fulkerson, Devil's Gate, Wyoming.
Photograph by Gregory M. Franzwa

Library of Congress Cataloging-in Publication Data

Graves and sites on the Oregon and California trails / edited by Randy
    Brown and Reg Duffin. — 2nd ed.
        p.   cm.
      Includes index.
      ISBN 0-9635901-9-7
      1. Tombs—Oregon Trail. 2. Tombs—California Trail. 3. Oregon
Trail—Antiquities. 4. California Trail—Antiquities. 5. Historic
sites—Oregon Trail. 6. Historic sites—California Trail.
I. Brown, Randy, 1947–   . II. Duffin, Reg. III. Oregon-California
Trails Association.
F597.G74   1998
917.950443—dc21   98-31429
                                                 CIP

Oregon-California Trails Association
P.O. Box 1019
Independence, MO, 64051-0519
816-252-2276

He was buried in his blanket, the camp furnishing no wood for a coffin The burial service was read over him . . . the dust and ashes scattered, and the first shovelful of earth thrown in . . . he was left in that wild solitude without even the silent companionship of the other dead around him. . . . There is a consolation in lying down to one's last sleep amidst kindred and friends, or even where some eye shall now and then light upon the sod that covers, but to lie there, with the howl of the wolf or the prairie wind alone to break the silence that broods over this green waste, is death indeed.

—George Gibbs, 1849

Randy Brown

W. H. Bedford - died July 4, 1852, age 28 years. Soda Hollow, Hastings Cutoff, Wyoming

Contents

viii   Contents

Foreword

A call came in late one afternoon in the late spring of 1982 from Bob Rennells, who then lived in La Grande, Oregon, at the base of Blue Mountains. "We've lost some more of the trail," he said. "Some guy plowed up those beautiful ruts west of Echo for a potato field."

Many Oregon Trail aficionados had been trying for years on their own to make people aware of the need to preserve the rapidly dwindling remnants of the greatest migration in American history, with no success. It occurred to Rennells and me that we might have a little more impact if we banded together to mount a preservation effort and to develop an education program to save what was left of the trails.

I asked a number of trail friends to join me in Denver, and that was the beginning of the Oregon-California Trails Association. Merrill J. Mattes, James F. Bowers, Roger Blair, Dr. John A. Latschar, Troy Gray, former Congressman Jim Johnson, and Rennells were among those who made that trip. By noon of August 11, 1982, the job was done. Modifications were made to the bylaws I had suggested, the name was chosen, and we were off and running. The sole purpose at that time was the preservation of the trails.

In May 1997 I drove the complete route of the Oregon National Historic Trail, from Independence, Missouri, to Oregon City, Oregon, for the first time since 1972. I was truly surprised at the impact of OCTA on the land. In desolate areas I saw some of the hundreds of diminutive white Carsonite fiberglass posts, emblazoned with the OCTA logo, which mark the ruts of the historic trails. I was pleasantly surprised to see so much of the trail remaining, on private as well as federal land. Ranchers seemed to be both proud and protective of the ruts that course through their property. Federal and state agencies, now aware that some people really care about the trail and its historic sites, found popular support for marking and other preservation efforts.

I was delighted to see that the Bureau of Land Management and the U.S. Forest Service were developing important sites along the trail. Now the American people are learning what happened at such places. I crossed the new bridge west of the Little Colorado Desert at the site of the old Lombard Ferry. There the BLM has erected an impressive array of interpretive panels, to teach us what happened at this important and dangerous crossing of the Green River. I toured the magnificent BLM installation atop Flagstaff Hill, to see the tears of visitors as they read of the hardships of the pioneers who crossed this desolate land. I visited the interpretive park at the Blue Mountain Crossing near La Grande, Oregon, and marveled at the way the U.S. Forest Service is leading visitors along the deep swales of the Oregon Trail. I toured the "Big Wagons" at Oregon City, shuddering as the crashing sound/light show depicted the raging Kansas thunderstorms that so bedeviled the pioneers.

There are many more such places along the Oregon-California Trails. Not one of the dramatic interpretive facilities has been sponsored by OCTA, but every one was in some way influenced by the members of our trail organization. The awareness created by OCTA had more than a little to do with making funding more available for such places. The involvement of OCTA members helped to ensure that the interpretation was accurate.

Several thousand emigrants died along the 2,000-mile journey to the West. One historian estimated that there is an average of one grave for every eighty yards of the trail. Most of their graves were obliterated immediately after burial, to protect them against human and animal predators. A few hundred graves are visible today, and the names of some of the victims are still identifiable. At the time OCTA was formed, a dozen or so were protected by steel pipe fencing. But more than 100 were not protected, and many were deteriorating, largely because of cattle rubbing.

In 1985 the veteran trail sleuth, Reg P. Duffin, of suburban Chicago, was asked to take charge of a graves protection effort. Duffin invited school teacher Randy Brown of Douglas, Wyoming, to join him in creating OCTA's Graves and Sites Committee after the two met during OCTA's Scottsbluff convention. Using outstanding research skills, they provided background information on the deceased, then arranged for a permanent marker, and sometimes protective fencing, to be installed at the grave sites. Their efforts were reported in OCTA's quarterly magazine, *Overland Journal*, so that members could be aware of the graves and their new markers. Duffin set the pattern for preservation which has been followed since.

More than sixty markers are in place now. Endangered headstones have been protected by rail fences.

OCTA's first *Graves and Sites* booklet was issued in 1991. It is hoped that this second edition will be the precursor to many more, as OCTA's work in grave preservation will not cease until every known grave along the Oregon-California Trail is marked and protected. That is the challenge that is faced not only by Reg Duffin and Randy Brown, but every single member of this vibrant organization. It is a challenge that will be met.

Gregory M. Franzwa
Tucson, Arizona

Preface to the Second Edition

Since the first publication of this book in 1991 the Graves and Sites Committee of OCTA has continued with its marking program. An additional twenty-five Nova-Color markers have been put up at graves and various other sites in seven trail states. OCTA chapters have also initiated some marking projects of their own. These projects have been a welcome and valuable new aspect of OCTA's preservation efforts. The chapter projects bring to thirty-two the total of newly marked sites which make up the bulk of the new material in this edition. Also, in a few instances some of the information from the first edition has been revised to reflect more recent research or updated ownership of sites and the directions for finding them. Marker texts remain unchanged, however. It is hoped that this expanded edition will be a valuable guide to the important historical sites that are described and will encourage OCTA members and others to visit them. That is the main purpose of this publication.

The Graves and Sites Committee has been assisted by many OCTA members in all stages of the marking projects new to this edition. The assistance may have been given in the research of texts, obtaining the consent of landowners, actually placing the markers at the sites, constructing fences, and in the preparation for the publication of this book. Many acknowledgments are given in the guides for each marker so there may be some repetition here.

For the Smith-Simonton marker, Ron Becher did the research and wrote the text, and Russ Genung helped put up the marker. Ron also contacted the landowner. For the Sarepta Gore Fly marker, Bob Wallace got permission to place the marker at the Plum Creek Cemetery, and Bill and Jan Hill of OCTA provided much needed assistance in the placing of the marker. At the Pierre Papin grave, Lee Underbrink helped with the fence and cooked steaks for dinner. The ones the dog didn't get were excellent. Joe McClenahan of Gering reinstalled the fragment of the original cross at the grave. For Robidoux Trading Post and Pass, the late Merrill Mattes wrote the texts and helped us to combat a certain office of the federal government during the project.

Reg and Dorothy Duffin visited William Clary's hometown in Missouri and provided additional information about him. Bill and Jan Hill finally located the Charles Bishop grave site for which I'd been searching for many years. Bob and Karen Rennells assisted in getting permission from the BLM to mark and fence the Lucinda B. Wright grave. Reg Duffin did the research that finally identified Lucinda Wright. At the Fulkerson grave, the fence was built by Dick Smith of Casper, and several members of the Wyoming Chapter helped install it and erect the marker. At Raft River, Larry Jones, John Davis, and Burt Silcock installed the marker just in time for the visit of the 1993 Oregon Trail commemorative wagon train. For Lucinda Duncan, Bob Pearce helped with the arrangements for placing the marker and organized a dedication ceremony with the Duncan descendants.

In Oregon, Lowell Tiller and Dick Ackerman did all the work at the Chambers and Koontz graves and for the Applegate Trail markers. They also very patiently provided me with the details needed for the pages on these markers. Al Mulder of the Utah

Crossroads Chapter provided the information on the kiosks that chapter has installed. The California-Nevada Chapter was responsible for the Bruff's Camp, Sonora, Grove Cook, and Lassen-Clapper markers. Tom Hunt and Don Buck provided directions to these sites and other comments for the descriptions. Pat Loomis sent more information on Grove Cook, which was added to the comments section for that grave site. For Nancy Kelsey, the landowner, Bonnie Goller, provided biographical material not otherwise available, while Philip Ault of Santa Maria did most of the research on which the marker text was based and promptly answered several inquiries.

Greg Franzwa and Betty Burnett helped with editing the marker texts and arranged the camera-ready layouts provided to the manufacturer, Nova-Color of Ogden, Utah. Jack Woods of Nova-Color was always ready to answer my questions and accommodated us several times when I asked that the marker on order be put on their "hurry up" priority list. The company never let OCTA down.

Jim Budde, OCTA treasurer, advised me on our marking program and got all the bills paid on time. Tom Hunt, OCTA's then National Preservation Officer, continued to offer his support and advice and spearheaded the California marking projects. Thanks also to the members of OCTA's board of directors, past and present, who took an interest in the marking program.

Susan Badger Doyle of OCTA's Publications Committee took charge of the publication of this edition and was our expert editor. Rose Ann Tompkins, also of the Publications Committee, did the layout work for the book on her Macintosh computer and got the new edition off the ground by basically telling me to get at it.

Reg Duffin, the first chairman of the Graves and Sites Committee, continued to work as a member of the committee and was the inspiration for most of the work that has been done in the last eight years since I took over as chairman.

Last of all, without the cooperation of the landowners, nearly all of them ranchers and farmers of the West, none of this work could have been done. Their good will and acceptance of OCTA's preservation efforts have made all this possible.

Randy Brown
Chairman, Graves and Sites Committee

Introduction

Before OCTA, preservation of emigrant graves on the Oregon-California Trail was primarily a personal effort. In Wyoming, for example, people have tended to the graves for years, and some graves have been protected by sturdy iron-pipe fencing that remains in excellent condition today, reflecting the efforts of individuals, Boy Scout troops, and local civic groups in maintaining these historical sites.

In the 1950s, Wyoming Historical Society emigrant trail treks led by L. C. Bishop, Albert Sims, Lyle Hildebrand, all of Douglas, Wyoming, and Paul Henderson of Bridgeport, Nebraska, focused statewide attention on historical trail sites, and pioneer graves became a matter of permanent record. Since that time, it may be fair to say, until OCTA's efforts the graves of the trail had suffered from neglect. By the 1980s they needed renewed maintenance and attention.

OCTA's Graves and Sites Committee was formed during the 1985 Scottsbluff convention, and incoming president Tom Hunt asked Reg Duffin of La Grange Park, Illinois, to become its first chairman. Randy Brown of Douglas, Wyoming, joined the committee later that summer. Earlier that year OCTA's first successful efforts at marking had resulted in the Paul Henderson memorial monument in Bridgeport, Nebraska; the fencing of the Joel Hembree grave in Wyoming; and the Narcissa Whitman marker (in cooperation with the state of Nebraska) on U.S. 26 east of Broadwater, Nebraska.

With the formation of the Graves and Sites Committee, inspired by the upcoming 1987 Casper convention, the work of researching, marking, and protecting Wyoming's trail graves began in earnest. With much to be done, Randy Brown recruited his students at Walker Creek School as assistants for the field work. Eventually the crew was reduced to two, fifth-graders Jim Rankin and Jacque Downs, and for a few years, on behalf of Reg Duffin and the committee, they accomplished most of the field work that was done under OCTA's sponsorship. Following the formation of the Trail Marking Committee by Bob Berry and Randy Brown, they placed the first OCTA Carsonite trail markers in 1988.

Lee Underbrink of Casper, Wyoming, who was the 1987 convention chairman, provided the committee and OCTA's board of directors with information about an aluminum, pedestal-type sign, manufactured by Nova-Color of Ogden, Utah. The dark brown plaques with gold lettering provided by Nova-Color became the standard OCTA marker for graves and sites. Fifty-two of these markers have been placed at trail sites, most of them graves, since 1987.

Research of the Graves and Sites Committee, in some instances aided by the local OCTA chapter, has resulted in much new information on trail graves being made available. Many graves previously identified with just a name, and sometimes not even that, now have a story that can be told about them and about the individual buried there. This has been an important aspect of the committee's work. Graves that have benefited from this research include William Clary, Henry Hill, Mily/Millie Irwin, Joel Hembree, Mary Hurley, Martin Ringo, Quintina Snodderly, Frederick Fulkerson,

Daniel Lantz, Nancy Hill, Lucinda B. Wright, Elizabeth Paul, Shepherd-Wright, Sanford Johnson, Ephraim Brown, and W. H. Bedford. The last three, for various reasons, have not been marked by OCTA. Articles on most of these graves, written by Reg Duffin or Randy Brown, have been published either in the *Overland Journal* or *News From the Plains*. In addition, Duffin's article on Lucinda Wright appeared in *The Annals of Wyoming*, and articles by Bill Hill on the Bishop grave and one by Amy Williams about the Charlotte Dansie grave appeared in the *Overland Journal*.

Scattered throughout the book are photographs of graves and gravestones of which little or nothing is known about the individual buried there. An appendix that includes such graves in Wyoming is in the back of the book.

The work of the Graves and Sites Committee will go on for many years. It was often thought that we would soon run out of graves to mark, but candidates have thus far continued to appear. Thousands of graves are on the trail but their exact locations remain unknown or unidentified. The precious few that have been identified, preserved, and memorialized by OCTA and others are just a small portion of the tens of thousands of emigrants who lost their lives on the trails to Oregon, California, and Utah. May we never forget them.

NEBRASKA

George Winslow

Randy Brown

General Comments - This revered grave of forty-niner George Winslow, discovered in the 1870s, has been carefully preserved by the land-owning Boddye family, including current owner Ed Boddye of Fairbury. OCTA's marker was installed in conjunction with the 1990 Omaha convention at a dedication ceremony held at the gravesite. OCTA member Estaline Carpenter was instrumental in gaining permission to place the marker and in gaining access to the site during the convention tour.

Location - About 4 miles north of Fairbury, Jefferson County, Nebraska. SW¼, Sec. 21, T3N, R2E.

Ownership
Ed Boddye
RFD 1
Fairbury, NE 68352
(402) 729-6040

Access - Open to the public.

Directions - From Fairbury, go north on Nebraska 15 for about 4 miles from its intersection with U.S. 136. Turn west on a gravel road. Proceed for about 1.5 miles to a gate into the pasture. If the gate is open, cars may be driven on the obvious lane to the gravesite. If the gate is closed, walk the easy ¼ mile to the site.

GEORGE WINSLOW

On April 16, 1849, the twenty-five members of the Boston-Newton Joint Stock Association left Boston, Massachusetts, to travel overland to the goldfields of California.

On May 29 at Soldier Creek, near present-day Topeka, Kansas, one of the founders of the Association, 25-year-old George Winslow, a machinist from Newton Upper Falls, was suddenly taken violently ill with cholera.

The company remained in camp for three days, and Winslow appeared to be recovering. Late in the afternoon of June 6 the company reached the point where the Oregon-California Trail crosses the present Nebraska-Kansas state line. There, David J. Staples, Winslow's brother-in-law, described a "terrific thunder shower, lightning flashed sometimes dazzling to the eyes. Rain falling in torrents." George Winslow's death probably resulted from exposure to this storm. At 9 A.M. on June 8, "painlessly as though going to sleep, he died."

"He was borne to the grave by eight bearers. The last chapter of Ecleasiastees was read." As a token of their respect each member of the company placed a green sprig on the grave.

A headstone inscribed GEO WINSLOW, NEWTON, MS AE 25 was set at the head of the grave. On a footstone the year "1849." The headstone is now incorporated in the granite monument.

Through the efforts of George W. Hanson of Fairbury, the state of Nebraska, and the sons of George Winslow, the granite monument was erected here and dedicated October 12, 1912.

There is at least one other emigrant grave on this ground between the forks of Whiskey Run Creek. On May 23, 1850, Elias Daggy wrote: "Travel 5 miles the road making several sprangles which now come together—where there are two graves—Geo. Winslow—Newton Mo. [Mass.] age 25—1849 & R. Depew—St. Louis Mo. died June 25th 1849 age 62."

Research, Signing and Funding by the: 1990

**OREGON-CALIFORNIA
TRAILS ASSOCIATION**

This is a part of your American heritage. Honor it, protect it, preserve it for your children.

Eubank Ranch Site

Gene Werner

General Comments - On August 7, 1864, Sioux, Cheyenne, and Arapaho war parties simultaneously raided along the Platte Road for more than 300 miles from Big Sandy Station to Julesburg. The ranches on the Little Blue River were all targeted. In the raid on the William Eubank ranch, located at the Narrows of the Little Blue, William Eubank and four other family members were killed. Five women and children were taken captive: Lucinda Eubank and her children Isabelle, three, and Will, nine months; her nephew Ambrose Asher, nine; and visiting neighbor Laura Roper, sixteen.

All the captives were eventually released: Laura Roper, Isabelle Eubank, and Ambrose Asher at a treaty council in Colorado, and Lucinda and Will Eubank at Fort Laramie. Isabelle died soon after her release, but the others survived and lived long lives. Lucinda Eubank's descendants and documentary evidence confirm the spelling

of the surname as Eubank, not Eubanks. And of particular interest to this project, prominent OCTA member Dave Welch is a descendant of Ambrose Asher, whom historians long thought had died soon after his release.

Location - Oak, Nuckolls County, Nebraska. SE¼NE¼, Sec. 6, T3W, R5W.

Ownership - Mr. Gene Werner.

Access - The marker can be read from the county road. Permission must be obtained to visit relevant sites located between the road and the river.

Directions - From the Oregon Trail Park in the center of Oak, drive approximately ½ mile west, then approximately 1 mile north. Note a white farm gate on the west side of the road. The marker is within the field.

THE EUBANKS RANCH - 1864

Continually dispossessed from their hunting grounds of time immemorial by the inevitability of the expanding frontier, the Indian tribes were pitted against settler and soldier for possession of territory, at times with untold fury and savagery.

In August, 1864, the Cheyenne, Sioux, and Arapahoe made concerted, well-organized attacks on stage stations and ranches along the Oregon-California Trail from Julesburg to the Big Sandy Station effectively stopping overland travel for two months.

Three-fourths of a mile west of here, at the Narrows area of the Oregon Trail, on the afternoon of August 7, 1864, Indians attacked and destroyed the William Eubanks ranch, killing seven members of the Eubanks family.

Mrs. Eubanks, her three-year-old daughter, Isabelle, and six-month-old son, along with sixteen-year-old Laura Roper, who was visiting the Eubanks at the time, were taken prisoner.

On September 11, 1864, Major Wynkoop, commander at Fort Lyon, Colorado, held a council with the Cheyenne and Arapahoe on Hackberry Creek, a south branch of the Smoky Hill River. At that time Laura Roper and Isabelle Eubanks were released by Cheyenne Chief Black Kettle and Left Hand of the Arapahoe tribe. Laura was later reunited with her family.

In May, 1865, Sioux chiefs Two Face and Blackfoot brought a demented Mrs. Eubanks and her son in to Fort Laramie. On May 16 both Indians were hung at the fort for alleged abuse of the captives. It is believed that Isabelle Eubanks was never reunited with her mother and was adopted by a Dr. Brondsall of Denver. Isabelle never recovered from her ordeal and died shortly thereafter.

In 1929 Laura Roper, then Mrs. Laura Vance of Oklahoma, returned here to the valley of the Little Blue to identify the site of the Eubanks Ranch and place of her capture. Markers now locate these sites.

Research Signing and Funding by the

August 1988

OREGON-CALIFORNIA TRAILS ASSOCIATION

This is a part of your American heritage. Honor it, protect it, preserve it for your children.

Attack on the Simonton-Smith Train

Randy Brown

The actual grave site is located along fence line near bushes above the marker.

General Comments - OCTA member Ron Becher of Lincoln, Nebraska, has written the definitive study of the attacks on wagon trains traveling the Oregon Trail in Nebraska during the Indian War of 1864. The text of this marker is one result of his work.

Location - South of Hastings, Adams County, Nebraska. NW¼, Sec. 24, T6N, R10W.

Directions - From the intersection of U.S. 6 and U.S. 281 south of Hastings, Nebraska, drive south on 281 for six miles. Turn left (east) on dirt Saddlehorn Road. (The sign identifying Saddlehorn is on the west side of the highway.) There is a large state Oregon Trail monument on the west side of U.S. 281 just before the intersection with Saddlehorn Road. Drive 0.4 miles east on Saddlehorn to reach the site of the marker on the south side of the road. To reach the marker via Nebraska 74, the approximate route of the trail from the east, drive north on U.S. 281 from the intersection with Nebraska 74. Saddlehorn Road is 3 miles north. In this case, turn right to reach the marker.

Access - The marker can be read from the county road right-of-way. Permission is required to visit the grave site.

Ownership - Adams County, Nebraska.

ATTACK ON THE SIMONTON-SMITH TRAIN

About 300 yards southeast of this point, the Oregon-California Trail traversed a wide ravine known locally as Indian Hollow—the scene of the first fatal action of the Indian War of 1864 in Nebraska Territory.

Enraged and bewildered by unprovoked attacks upon their people in Colorado Territory, the Southern Cheyenne and Arapahoe tribes determined to focus their revenge on the busy Oregon-California Trail. From advance camps on the Republican River, they fanned out to strike the route between present Hebron and the Platte River at the Adams-Kearney County line, a section of the road long considered to be peaceful and secure.

On the hot Sunday morning of August 7, the Indians ambushed a small train of six wagons crossing Indian Hollow. The train, owned by Thomas Simonton of Denver, was returning from St. Joseph, Missouri, under the leadership of Horace G. Smith. The cargo included a threshing machine, hardware, iron stoves, crockery, and foodstuffs, most of which was consigned to George Tritt, a Denver merchant. Five of the drivers were killed instantly by arrows. The sixth, with one arrow embedded in his forehead and another in his body, crawled into hiding in a field of tall sunflowers at the bottom of the hollow. The frightened horses and mules pulled the wagons up out of the ravine where the Indians cut them free of their harnesses. The wagons were ransacked and set ablaze, though not all of them burned completely.

Early on Monday morning, August 8, George Comstock and Overland Stage Line employees from Thirty-Two Mile Station arrived on the scene. They found the wounded teamster, who related a few details of the attack before he died. The six men were buried on the ridge beside the trail, about 140 yards south of this point. They were the first victims of the great raids of August 7, 1864, which took at least forty-eight lives in Nebraska Territory.

The monument at the grave site was provided by Hastings Boy Scouts and was dedicated on Sunday, May 17, 1931, before a crowd of 300 local citizens.

Signing and Funding by

OREGON-CALIFORNIA TRAILS ASSOCIATION

1996

This is a part of your American heritage. Honor it, protect it, preserve it for your children.

The Plum Creek Massacre

Randy Brown

General Comments - The site of the graves of the victims of this Indian attack is in the hayfield on the opposite side (south) of the road from the location of this marker. This ground has never been plowed.

Ron Becher of Lincoln, Nebraska, has researched the Indian War of 1864 and has provided previously unknown information about the Plum Creek Massacre. His book on the subject will appear in 1999.

Location - South of Overton, Phelps County, Nebraska. Overton is approximately 10 miles east of Lexington. SW¼, Sec. 10, T8N, R20W.

Directions - From the I-80 Overton Exit, drive south across the Platte for about 2.5 miles. Then turn west on a paved county road and drive approximately 2 miles to the site of the marker on north side of the road.

Access - Open to the public.

Ownership - Phelps County, Nebraska.

THE PLUM CREEK MASSACRE

On the morning of August 8, 1864, a war party of Cheyenne and Arapaho Indians attacked a Denver-bound freight wagon train killing thirteen men and taking captive Nancy Jane Morton of Sidney, Iowa, and nine-year old Daniel Marble of Council Bluffs, Iowa.

The wagon train consisted of twelve wagons from three outfits. Six of the wagons were reportedly from St. Joseph, Missouri, and carried shelled corn and farm implements. Three wagons, loaded with hardware and foodstuffs, were owned by William D. Marble of Council Bluffs. The remaining three were owned by Thomas Frank Morton. Accompanying Morton were his wife, Nancy Jane; her brother William Fletcher; and a cousin, John Fletcher.

The attack scattered the wagons on this site. Some turned toward the river, while others turned southward toward the bluffs. All thirteen men in the combined outfits were killed. Mrs. James Smith, of Marble's outfit, was traveling far advance with her husband and his partner. She escaped by hiding in a cattail marsh near the river.

The attack took place in full view of several east-bound freight trains and a small detachment of soldiers of the Seventh Iowa Cavalry who were stopped at the Thomas Ranch a mile and a half west of this site. From the telegraph station at the ranch Lt. Joseph Bone sent a frantic message for help to Fort Kearny, about thirty-five miles east: "Send company of men here quick as God can send them one hundred Indians in sight firing on ox train." The troops did not arrive until ten o'clock that night.

The victims were buried the following morning. Eleven bodies were scattered about this area and were buried in a common grave in the field a few yards south of here. Lt. F. G. Comstock wrote: " . . . we buried the eleven men in a long trench but nothing had molested [the] dead previous to our arrival."

From varied accounts a partial list of the victims can be compiled: James Smith, a Mr. St. Clair, Charles Iliff, William D. Marble, Thomas Frank Morton, William Fletcher, John Fletcher, and six unidentified teamsters. The grave was described as being "upon the roadside in a mound slightly elevated and partly surrounded by a ravine."

In early September, Cheyenne Chief Black Kettle purchased Danny Marble and three other young people captured along the Little Blue and released them to Major Edward Wynkoop, of the First Colorado Cavalry, in northwestern Kansas. While awaiting return to his mother in Council Bluffs, Danny contracted typhoid fever. He died in Denver on November 9. According to legend, Mrs. James Smith died insane at Fort Kearny a few weeks after the massacre.

Nancy Morton, wounded by two arrows, remained a captive until about January 18, 1865, when she was ransomed by traders sent into the upper Powder River county of Wyoming by Major John Wood of the Seventh Iowa Cavalry. From Fort Laramie Nancy Morton returned over the trail to Fort Kearny and then took the stage to Nebraska City. She passed directly by this site where her family and friends had been murdered a few months earlier. She later wrote that being at the common grave brought back "the memory of that fatal morning repeatedly before me, not as a picture, but a present reality." She reached her father's home in Sidney on March 9, 1865, later remarried, and lived until 1912.

The story of Nancy Morton's captivity became known through her written manuscripts acquired from her granddaughter by local historian Clyde Wallace, who began his study of the Plum Creek area in 1930. The manuscripts are now in possession of the Dawson County Historical Society in Lexington.

Signing and Funding by

OREGON-CALIFORNIA TRAILS ASSOCIATION
1998

This is a part of your American heritage. Honor it, protect it, preserve it for your children.

Sarepta Gore Fly

Randy Brown

Randy Brown

General Comments - The actual site of Sarepta Fly's grave is no longer known, but the headstone that once marked her grave now lies in Plum Creek Cemetery. The OCTA marker stands next to it. Former OCTA Director Bill Hill and his wife Jan assisted in the installation of the marker. For more details, see Russ Czaplewski, *Captive of the Cheyenne* (Lexington, Nebr.: Dawson County Historical Society, 1993).

Location - South of Overton, Dawson County, Nebraska. SE¼, Sec. 8, T6N, R20W.

Directions - Follow the directions to the Plum Creek Massacre marker. Plum Creek Cemetery is approximately 2 miles west of the marker.

Access - Open to the public.

Ownership - Dawson County, Nebraska.

SAREPTA GORE FLY

The exact location of the Sarepta Fly grave is unknown. The headstone marking her grave was discovered early this century by children playing in a field on the old Dilworth Ranch, not far from this location. It had been covered by prairie grasses and was found half-buried in an animal burrow.

Sarepta Gore, the daughter of James Gore of Andrew County, Missouri, was born January 6,1841. In 1857 she married William Fly, a twenty-seven-year-old native of Howard County, Missouri. Fly went to the California gold mines in 1852 and remained there for five years. Sarepta and William were married upon his return to Missouri. The Flys soon took up farming in Kansas, but after three years there they joined the Colorado gold rush and crossed the plains to a Rocky Mountain mining town.

In 1865 the Fly family decided to return to Missouri. By this time William and Sarepta were the parents of three children: Carey B., born December 14,1858; John Davis, born October 12,1860; and James M., born April 21,1863. When the family reached the Plum Creek area, Sarepta died. According to family tradition, her death was sudden and unexpected, and the exact cause is unknown. The date, as revealed on the gravestone, was June 16,1865. A local legend says that William returned years later with the headstone to mark his wife's grave, carrying it in a wheelbarrow from Kearney, but like other similar wheelbarrow stories, this one is probably pure myth.

William Fly settled in Montana, where he again took up mining and later ranching. He remarried in 1872 and became a prominent citizen of the Bozeman area, where he died in December 1887.

The Sarepta Fly headstone was moved to this location in 1930 in preparation for the dedication of the Plum Creek Massacre marker and cemetery. The only actual burial within this cemetery plot, however, is that of a small, unidentified child whose remains were discovered on a farm near Loomis, Nebraska. The reinterment took place in 1963.

Research for this sign by the Dawson County Historical Society

Signing and Funding by

OREGON-CALIFORNIA TRAILS ASSOCIATION

1995

This is a part of your American heritage. Honor it, protect it, preserve it for your children.

Headstones of two Kansas graves. These graves do not have OCTA markers. Nothing is known about Attebery or Mastin.

D. Attebery - died May 31, 1849. Headstone now at Hollenberg Ranch House Museum, Kansas.

Thomas Mastin - died May 13, 1853. Headstone on St. Joe Road, west of Big Blue River crossing.

California Hill Marker

Location - West of Brule, Keith County, Nebraska. SW corner, Sec. 14, T13N, R41W.

Ownership
Oregon-California Trails Association
P.O. Box 1019
Independence, MO 64051-0519
(816) 252-2276

Access - Open to the public.

Directions - The marker is located on the north side of U.S. 30, approximately 4.5 miles west of Brule, Nebraska.

Randy Brown

CALIFORNIA HILL

The large hill to the north, which became known as "California Hill," was climbed by thousands of emigrants heading west during the covered wagon migrations, 1841–60. Many were bound for Oregon. California became the destination of a majority of travelers after gold was discovered there in 1848.

The most important crossing of the South Platte River during this period was south and a little east of here. After fording the river and ascending California Hill, the emigrants traveled northwesterly to the North Platte River via Ash Hollow. The terrain restricted the route wagons could take up the hill, causing deep ruts that are still visible about two-thirds of a mile north-north-west of this marker.

California Hill and this marker were gifts to the Oregon-California Trails Association by Malcolm E. Smith, Jr. in memory of Irene D. Paden who dedicated much of her life to retracing and writing about the Oregon and California Trails. The acquisition was facilitated by the generous cooperation of Ivor D. and Carol A. Dilky, the Farmers Home Administration, and the Adams Bank and Trust.

Oregon-California Trails Association
Nebraska State Historical Society

Rachel E. Pattison

Randy Brown

General Comments - Little is known about this well-known emigrant grave. The late W. W. Morrison of Cheyenne, Wyoming, is credited with uncovering the story of Rachel Pattison by contacting relatives in Oregon during months of persistent work, but little of the pertinent information has been published. Morrison then spearheaded the fund-raising drive for the stone monument that now encloses the original headstone. This monument was dedicated on the centennial anniversary of Rachel's death, on June 19, 1949. OCTA's marker was placed at the grave in June 1990 with the permission and assistance of Mrs. Frances Delatour, Secretary-Treasurer of the Ash Hollow Cemetery District, and Dennis Shimmin, superintendent of Ash

Hollow State Historical Park. For more information, see the May 1987 issue of *News From the Plains*.

Location - Ash Hollow Cemetery, Lewellen, Garden County, Nebraska. NW¼, Sec. 3, T15N, R42W.

Ownership - Ash Hollow Cemetery District.

Access - Open to the public.

Directions - Ash Hollow Cemetery is on the west side of U.S. 26, ¼ mile south of the bridge over the North Platte River outside Lewellen.

RACHEL E. PATTISON

"Rachel taken sick in the morning, died in the night." Thus did twenty-three-year-old Nathan Pattison record the death of his wife of two months, Rachel Warren Pattison.

Nathan and Rachel were married April 3, 1849, in Randolph County, Illinois. They left their homes near Sparta just one week later to take the trail to Oregon. Their company consisted primarily of Nathan's immediate family: his parents, William and Mary; five brothers; and William's aunt, Charlotte Irwin. Nathan's brother James was accompanied by his wife, Jane, and their infant son. With the Pattisons were some relatives of Jane Pattison named Wylie.

On June 18 the company reached Ash Hollow by way of Cedar Bluffs. The day before, they had lost three oxen that had eaten poisonous weeds, and William planned an early stop to do some repair work and to harness four mules to take the place of the remaining oxen. William Pattison's diary for June 19 is as follows:

"next day our Company left us about 11 ocl Rachel was taken with Colara and died by 11 at night of 19 instant   Medical aid was obtained from a train from Mechigan of the Dr Ormsby after burying on the left side of the hollow as you go round the bluff up the River on the second bank placing a gravestone at her head   Rachel Pattison aged 18 June 19th 1849."

The man who tended Rachel in her final hours was Dr. Caleb N. Ormsby of Ann Arbor.

Charlotte Irwin died on October 12 as the company crossed the Blue Mountains. The Pattisons reached the Dalles of the Columbia on November 3. An attempt was made to raft down the river but an early winter storm left them stranded at the Cascades. After many days of privation they finally reached Fort Vancouver late in the month. The Pattisons spent the winter there while the men of the company cut timber for the fort to earn their living. They went on to Oregon City in the spring of 1850.

Nathan Pattison never remarried and lived with his brother James and family for most of the rest of his life at various places in Oregon and Washington. He died near Olympia in 1893 and is buried in the Odd Fellows Cemetery in that city.

Research, Signing and Funding by the:

OREGON-CALIFORNIA TRAILS ASSOCIATION

In cooperation with the Ash Hollow Cemetery District

1990

This is a part of your American heritage. Honor it, protect it, preserve it for your children.

John Hollman Grave Site

General Comments - Nothing is known of John Hollman. The inscription on the headstone is almost illegible. A nearby State of Nebraska Oregon Trail marker is in part inscribed, "JOHN HOLLMAN DIED JUNE 5 1852." The Hollman grave was included in two listings of "emigrant deaths on the plains" published in newspapers in the fall of 1852. One reveals his point of origin as Missouri; the other gives his age as nineteen.

Because of undercutting erosion of the west bank of the knoll, the headstone has been reset in a more central position over the grave.

Ownership
Sylvia Tinkham
Box 343
Oshkosh, NE 69154
(308) 772-3729

Leased to - Chris and Ed Jasnock.

Access - Open to the public.

Location - South of Oshkosh, Garden County, Nebraska. NW¼, Sec. 10, T16N, R44W.

Directions - Drive south on Nebraska 27 from Oshkosh. Cross the North Platte River bridge, then turn right onto a graveled county road. Drive 0.1 mile west and the John Hollman grave is to the right (north) atop a knoll.

Nebraska State Historical Society

1924

Randy Brown

Note growth of timber since the 1924 photo was taken.

Narcissa Whitman Marker

Randy Brown

Location - East of Ancient Bluff Ruins on the north side of Platte River, on the north-side route of the Oregon-California Trail.

Ownership - State of Nebraska.

Access - Open to the public.

Directions - The marker is located 6 miles east of Broadwater, Morrill County, Nebraska, on the north side of U.S. 26.

NARCISSA WHITMAN

Narcissa Whitman, trail-blazer and martyred missionary, is one of the great heroines of the frontier West. In 1836 she and Eliza Spalding, following the north side of the Platte on horseback, became the first white women to cross the American continent.

The Protestant "Oregon Mission" was composed of Dr. Marcus Whitman, Rev. Henry Spalding, their new brides and William Gray. The traveled from New York to Otoe Indian Agency (Bellevue, Nebraska), then joined an American Fur Company caravan led by Thomas Fitzpatrick. From the Green River rendezvous they journeyed westward with traders of the Hudson's Bay Company. In November, 1847, Narcissa, her husband, and eleven others, were murdered by Cayuse Indians at their Walla Walla mission, now a National Historic Site.

The missionaries passed this point in June, 1836. In May, 1847 the Mormon Pioneers passed here en route from Winter Quarters (present North Omaha) to Salt Lake Valley, calling these formations "Ancient Bluff Ruins." Beginning with the California Gold Rush in 1849, this "Mormon Pioneer Trail" became "the Council Bluffs Road" to emigrants bound for the West Coast.

Courtesy of Elizabeth Hildebrand

Placing the U.S. military headstone at the Ralston Baker grave, Converse County, Wyoming, in 1955. Left to right: Albert Sims, unknown, Glen Edwards, Mrs. Edwards and child, Paul Henderson, L. C. Bishop, Lyle Hildebrand. See "Joel Hembree and Ralston Baker Grave Sites," pp. 44–45.

Paul C. Henderson Memorial Monument

Dorothy Duffin

Location - West of Bridgeport, Morrill County, Nebraska

Ownership - City of Bridgeport, Nebraska.

Access - Open to the public.

Directions - The monument is located at the entrance to the Oregon Trail Memorial Cemetery, on the north side of U.S. 26, west of Bridgeport, Nebraska.

IN MEMORY OF
PAUL C. HENDERSON
OF BRIDGEPORT, NEBRASKA
1895-1979

HONORED HISTORIAN AND MAP MAKER
OF THE OREGON-CALIFORNIA TRAIL
WHICH PASSED THIS WAY.
WITH HIS WIFE, HELEN, HE EXPLORED
AND RECORDED TRAIL REMAINS
AND SHARED HIS KNOWLEDGE
WITH A LEGION OF TRAIL FOLLOWERS.

DEDICATED AUGUST 17, 1985

 **OREGON-CALIFORNIA
TRAILS ASSOCIATION**

Pierre Didier Papin

Randy Brown

General Comments - The site of the Pierre D. Papin grave is still marked by a fragment of the large wooden cross that was erected over the grave in 1853. This fragment has been stabilized with a support post set in place by Joe McClenahan of Gering. The fence around the grave was built by Randy Brown of the Graves and Sites Committee and OCTA Director Lee Underbrink. The text of the marker is based on research done by William Goff, as published in LeRoy Hafen's series *Mountain Men and the Fur Trade*. A large stone monument approximately ¼ mile southwest of the grave marks the site of the fur company's Fort John. For more details on the grave, see Gregory M. Franzwa, *Maps of the Oregon Trail* (Gerald, Mo.: The Patrice Press, 1982): 102; and "Pierre D. Papin Gravesite Rediscovered," *Overland Journal* 1, no. 2 (Fall 1983): 36-37.

Location - South of Gering, Scottsbluff County, Nebraska. NE¼, Sec. 6, T20N, R55W.

Directions - From the intersection of Nebraska 92 and Nebraska 71, west of Gering, drive south on Nebraska 71 for 5.5 miles and then turn right (west) on County Road W. In 1 mile at a T intersection, turn left on County Road 20. The Papin grave is approximately 0.5 mile beyond this intersection on a knoll to the left of the road. The site is found shortly after crossing an irrigation ditch on a wooden bridge.

Access - Open to the public.

Ownership
Marjorie Schleicher
1610 Ave. I
Scottsbluff, NE 69361
(308) 635-1183

PIERRE DIDIER PAPIN

P. D. Papin was a trusted and valued employee of the American Fur Company and its successors for over thirty years. He was born March 7, 1798, in St. Louis. The Papins were a prominent French merchant family in that city.

Papin joined "the Company" in the early 1820s and worked with its Upper Missouri Outfit headquartered in present-day South Dakota. Papin established his own trading company in 1829 but was soon bought out by the American Fur Company, which then rehired him. By 1842 Papin had moved to Fort John (popularly known as Fort Laramie) on the Laramie River and in 1845 became chief agent at that post. Meanwhile, the company had reorganized as Pierre Chouteau Jr. & Co., but operations remained essentially unchanged.

On June 15, 1846, Papin was met by Francis Parkman on the Platte River in Nebraska while enroute to St. Louis with a load of fur.

"The boats, eleven in number, deep-laden with the skins, hugged close to the shore. . . . Papin sat in the middle of one of the boats, upon the canvas that protected the cargo. He was a stout, robust fellow, with a little gray eye, that had a peculiarly sly twinkle. . . . I shook hands with the bourgeois, *and delivered the letter: then the boats swung around into the stream and floated away."*

Upon arrival in St. Louis the company granted Papin a partnership. In 1848 while in St. Louis he refused to return to Laramie and was succeeded at that post by Andrew Drips. However, by 1851 Papin was back on the frontier and still with "the Company."

In 1849 Fort Laramie was purchased by the U.S. Army and Drips established a company trading post here in Helvas Canyon. Papin was at this post with the company's Fort John Outfit when he died in May 1853. He was buried here, his grave marked by a large cedar cross.

Papin was survived by his wife, Catherine, and four children. There were twenty-six grandchildren.

Research by William A. Goff, Kansas City, Mo.

Signing and Funding by   1991

OREGON-CALIFORNIA
TRAILS ASSOCIATION

This is a part of your American heritage. Honor it, protect it, preserve it for your children.

Robidoux Trading Post

Randy Brown

General Comments - The actual site of Robidoux's establishment remains unmarked, but its location can be viewed from the knoll where the marker stands. OCTA founder Merrill Mattes spearheaded the placement of this marker and the one overlooking Robidoux Pass. A dedication ceremony for both markers was held in summer 1994 at which Mattes was the featured speaker. Randy Brown constructed the fence around the grave to protect the marker from grazing cattle. Contrary to the marker's text, the trail crossing of the adjacent ravine is still visible, although the ravine has eroded to a great depth at that point. Visitors to the site are encouraged to hike up the hill behind the marker to inspect this interesting trail remnant. The route is marked by OCTA's Carsonite trail markers. From the ravine crossing, the trail can be followed to a fence line. A few feet down the fence is the approximate spot of the Dunn grave of 1849.

Location - West of Gering, Scottsbluff County, Nebraska. SE¼, Sec. 7, T21N, R56W.

Directions - From the intersection of Nebraska 92 and Nebraska 71 travel south for 2.5 miles and turn west on paved Carter Canyon Road. (Avoid rough, dusty, or muddy Robidoux Pass Road.) In approximately 6 miles, turn right on County Road 15, then left in another mile. You are then on Robidoux Pass Road. The trail crosses this road in 1.9 miles. The marker is on the knoll to the left at that point. It is next to an older stone marker put up in about 1940. Directions from the Papin grave: return to the intersection with County Road W, continue north for 3 miles, and then turn left on Cedar Canyon Road. Travel 5 miles west and then turn right on County Road 15 to reach Robidoux Pass Road in 1 mile.

Access - Open to the public.

Ownership
Ernest Ouderkirk
160085 Ouderkirk Dr.
Gering, NE 69341
(308) 436-5195

ROBIDOUX TRADING POST

In 1849 Joseph Robidoux III of St. Joseph, Missouri, licensed in the Indian trade, ordered removal of his outfit from the vicinity of Fort Laramie to this strategic pass over Scotts Bluff, where there was ample wood and water. Evidence from several emigrant diaries, together with artifacts found at the site, confirm the location of his new post at a point about 300 yards north-northeast of here at the intersection of the big spring-fed ravine to your right, flowing north, and the smaller drainage descending eastward from the crest of the pass.

The trading post and its relation to the two ravines is noted in the 1850 journal of Capt. Howard Stansbury while traveling eastward: *"Scotts Bluffs—at a small rivulet, row of old deserted houses. [Also] spring at foot of the Sandstone Bluffs, where the [emigrant] road crosses the ridge."*

The ruts of the Oregon-California Trail approaching from the east are still clearly visible as they ascend toward the head of the ravine, at the foot of the bluff behind you. However, erosion has obliterated evidence of the actual crossing of the ravine.

In 1850 Robidoux's place is described by James Bennett as *"a row of rudely constructed huts composed of cedar logs and mud,"* serving as a trading post or store, blacksmith shop, and dwellings, usually surrounded by tipis occupied by Indian families of the Robidoux clan. The principal ones identified by emigrants were son Joseph Robidoux IV and nephew Antoine Robidoux.

Since the original intention of the Robidoux family was to trade with the Indians for buffalo robes, they were probably at first dismayed by the sudden invasion of their domain by a large army of covered-wagon emigrants bound for the California goldfields. However, they seem to have adjusted rapidly to this development. The traders did a land-office business with the emigrants, principally in providing blacksmith services, though there was also a brisk trade in staples and whiskey. Another bonanza for the traders was the frequent abandonment of wagons and surplus gear and supplies by overloaded emigrants, which added to the Robidoux inventory.

Despite this unexpected prosperity, for whatever reason, in late 1850 the Robidoux family abandoned their trading post here and built a new one about one mile to the southeast, over the bluffs, in a place now called Carter Canyon, which was rarely visited by emigrants and probably soon abandoned. A famous visitor to the Carter Canyon site was Father Pierre Jean DeSmet in the autumn of 1851, following the great gathering of Indian tribes at Horse Creek during negotiations for the first Fort Laramie peace treaty. During the early 1851 emigration season the Robidoux Pass post was reopened to trade with the emigrants. However, later that season the Robidoux family finally abandoned the pass altogether and established posts on the trail at points both east and west of Scotts Bluff, the former at the fork in the trail near present Melbeta, the latter where the two trail branches rejoin at Horse Creek, near present Lyman, Nebraska.

Research, Funding, and Signing by the

OREGON-CALIFORNIA TRAILS ASSOCIATION

1994

Robidoux Pass

Randy Brown

General Comments - This marker is the companion to the Robidoux Trading Post marker. Both were put up as part of a project initiated by Merrill Mattes. The fence around the marker was built by Randy Brown. From the marker the trail can be seen as a deep swale topping the pass and beginning the descent on the western side. This trail segment is marked by OCTA's Carsonite trail markers. Far in the distance Laramie Peak can be seen on clear days. The view is the same one enjoyed by the covered-wagon emigrants. For more information on both Robidoux markers, see the October 1994 issue of *News From the Plains*.

Location - West of Gering, Scottsbluff County, Nebraska. SE¼, Sec. 6, T21N, R57W.

Directions - From the Robidoux Trading Post marker site, continue on Robidoux Pass Road to the top of the pass. In the middle of a wide left turn in 1.5 miles, there is a two-track ranch road that continues approximately west and leads to

the fence and marker in about 0.1 mile. On the way to this site watch for trail markers to the right of the road that mark the multiple swales of the trail climbing to the top of the pass. From this marker one can continue west without returning to Gering. To do so, return to Robidoux Pass Road. Turn right. In 0.6 mile turn right to continue on Robidoux Pass Road. After 5 miles turn right on paved Stegall Road. Travel 4.5 miles to Stegall and turn left on Nebraska 92. Reach Lyman, Nebraska, in 8 miles. Use 10th Ave. north out of Lyman to reach U.S. 26 at Henry, Nebraska, in about 6.5 miles. See directions to the Henry Hill grave, which is located south of the river near Henry. Alternately, one can continue west on Nebraska 92 from Lyman and reach U.S. 85 south of Torrington, Wyoming, in about 15 miles. If one chooses this route, see the directions to the William Clary grave site, which is near the junction of Nebraska 92 and U.S. 85.

Access - Open to the public.

ROBIDOUX PASS

Robidoux Pass was named for Joseph Robidoux III of St. Joseph, Missouri, who established a trading post and blacksmith shop here in 1849, just in time to witness the beginning of the great California gold rush.

This pass is an integral part of the original historic U-shaped Scotts Bluff, described by forty-niner William Kelly as being in the form of a horizontal shepherd's crook, with the present Wildcat Hills as the straight staff, Robidoux Pass as the top of the crook, and the climactic formations within present Scotts Bluff National Monument as the flair at the end of the crook.

This pass was used by Rocky Mountain fur trappers and traders who, in 1830, took the first wheeled vehicles westward along the Platte River, and by emigrants bound for Oregon beginning in 1843. It was also the classic route during the first two years of the California gold rush, 1849–50. However, evidence given by Capt. Howard Stansbury of the U.S. Corps of Topographical Engineers proves that, beginning in 1851, the great majority of emigrants along the south side of the North Platte River switched from Robidoux Pass to the V-shaped gap now called Mitchell Pass, within the present national monument, northeast of here.

Despite the preponderant use of Mitchell Pass in the later period, the evidence supported by emigrant diaries and military observers is that the Robidoux Pass route was never altogether abandoned. The eastern junction of these alternate routes was at a point this side of present Melbeta. They rejoined at Horse Creek, near present Lyman, Nebraska. Despite the apparent impression that the Mitchell Pass route was shorter and therefore preferable, measured tracings of the two routes on USGS quadrangle maps indicate that they were nearly equal in length.

Several factors make Robidoux Pass historically unique. The eastern approach, surrounded by picturesque bluffs, seemed to the struggling emigrants like an "enchanted valley." In the pass itself there were copious springs, described as among the best along the entire route to California, and nearby trees for firewood and wagon repairs. From the pass looking east is a spectacular view of the North Platte Valley and distant fairy-like Chimney Rock. From the summit of the pass the emigrants, looking west toward the sanctuary of Fort Laramie, got a magnificent panoramic view climaxed by Laramie Peak, mistakenly thought by some to be their first view of the Rocky Mountains.

Research, Funding, and Signing by the
OREGON-CALIFORNIA TRAILS ASSOCIATION
1994

This is a part of your American heritage. Honor it, protect it, preserve it for your children.

Ownership
Curtis Bennett
1450 Gentry Blvd.
Gering, NE 69341
436-4663

Additional Comments - A site well worth a visit is the reconstruction of the 1851 Carter Canyon Robidoux Post. From the Robidoux Pass marker, return to Robidoux Pass Road and turn right. In 0.6 mile reach the intersection noted above but do not turn. Continue straight ahead. The road is sandy and winds around for about 3.1 miles to Carter Canyon Road again. Turn left. The reconstructed post is 1.5 miles farther. From there one can continue east and north on Carter Canyon Road and return to Nebraska 71 and Gering. To go west toward Torrington, return 1.5 miles, turn right, and then left on Robidoux Pass Road in 3.1 miles. Follow the directions above to reach Lyman, Nebraska.

Four unidentified graves, now fenced and marked by a large granite boulder. Robidoux Pass, Nebraska. Photographer unknown. 1930s.

Wyoming State Archives

Irving Tilgner

Sanford Johnson - died May 26, 1850. Adjacent to Rachel Pattison at Ash Hollow, Nebraska.

A. Kelly - died July 14, 1852. Located two miles west of Ash Hollow, Nebraska.

Randy Brown

WYOMING

Henry Hill Grave

Randy Brown

Henry Hill gravesite circa 1950.
Source unknown.

General Comments - The text on the Henry Hill marker is based primarily on the interpretation of the inscription on a headstone found at the gravesite by OCTA's Aubrey L. Haines in 1972. The indistinct inscription is believed to read "HENRY HILL JUNE 8th 1852 AGED 59."

In June 1988 Randy Brown, researching at the University of Missouri, Columbia, found a list of burials on the plains between Independence, Missouri, and Fort Laramie, prepared by John H. Hays and published in the *St. Joseph Gazette,*

December 1, 1852. The names are listed in an east-west sequence, with the second to last entry being "Henry Hill Mo. June 8 aged 49." The original printing of this list was in the *Sacramento Union*, October 9, 1852. Here the entry for this grave reads "Henry Hill, of Missouri, died June 8, 1852, age 59 years." The discrepancy in Hill's age is probably a typographical error that occurred when the *St. Joseph Gazette* reprinted the story. The *Union* article confirms Haines' 1972 interpretation of the headstone inscription.

HENRY HILL

At least three grave markers, each with conflicting data, have marked this grave of Henry Hill. A wood headboard was found here in the 1870s. In 1972 a headstone was found among the stone debris inscribed HENRY HILL June 8 [?] 1852 59 M.

From the date of his death and numeral 59, presumed to be his age at death, it is believed that this is indeed the grave of Henry Hill, born in Caroline County, Virginia, in 1793. A veteran of the War of 1812, he sold 399 acres of land in Monroe County, Missouri, in April 1852, to accompany his daughters, Martha and Clemencia, and son Joseph Littleton Hill, with their families to California.

From the North Platte ferry area, on June 15, 1852, in-law James Hill wrote: "...about thirty five miles below Fort Larame we was called on to pay the last tribute of respect to old Father Hill." The cause of death was a cholera-like illness. "next morning we buried little black boy Billy."

Henry's daughter, Clemencia, died on the Forty-mile Desert in Nevada. Nancy J. Hill, the sister-in-law of his son, Joseph, died July 5,1852, on the Sublette Cutoff. Her marked grave is located northwest of Kemmerer, Wyoming.

Research by

MRS. MARILYN HILL CRAIG
and the

OREGON-CALIFORNIA TRAILS ASSOCIATION

Funding by

MRS. MARILYN HILL CRAIG
McMinnville, Oregon
(Great-great-granddaughter of Henry Hill)

1987

This is a part of your American heritage. Honor it, protect it, preserve it for your children.

For additional information, see Reg Duffin, "The Nancy Hill Story: The Final Chapter," *Overland Journal* 4, no. 4 (Fall 1986): 56-64.

Location - Two miles southwest of Henry, Nebraska, in Goshen County, Wyoming. NW¼, Sec. 9, T23N, R60W.

Ownership
Gary Nickal
Nickal Brothers Farms
118 Arrowhead Road
Torrington, WY 82240
(307) 532-4770

Leased to
Adam and Teresa Cross
RR2 Box 317A
Torrington, WY 82240
(307) 532-4542

Access - Permission is required to visit the site.

Directions - From Henry, Nebraska, drive 2 miles south on highway L79C, 1¼ miles west, ¾ mile north to ranch area, ½ mile west.

Charles B. Bishop

Randy Brown

General Comments - The grave of forty-niner Charles Bishop is located on the same bluff, called Jamison Bluff, as the grave of William Clary. The graves are about a mile apart. This grave was located by Bill and Jan Hill of New York. Randy Brown built the fence around the grave. For more information on the Bishop grave, see William Hill, "Charles Bishop Grave Discovered" *Overland Journal* 7, no. 1 (1989): 29-32.

Location - South of Torrington, Goshen County, Wyoming. NW¼, Sec. 32, T24N, R60W.

Directions - Same as for the grave of William L. Clary.

Access - Permission is required to visit the site.

Ownership
Gary Nickal
118 Arrowhead Rd.
Torrington, WY 82240
(307) 532-4770

Leased to
Adam and Teresa Cross
RR2 Box 317A
Torrington, WY 82240
(307) 532-4542

CHARLES B. BISHOP

Charles B. Bishop was a member of the Washington City and California Gold Mining Association, a forty-niner gold rush company captained by J. Goldsborough Bruff. Bishop died July 8,1949, while encamped with his company near the river below this hill.

Of Bishop virtually nothing is known. He is listed in the company roster as a twenty-five-year-old citizen of Washington, D.C., and according to Bruff was a veteran of the Mexican War. Many members of the company were federal employees and perhaps young Bishop had worked as a clerk in a government office. On April 2, 1849, he left the city with his companions and headed for Pittsburgh, where they would board steamboats for St. Louis and then St. Joseph. From there they would take the trail to California.

Of Sunday morning, July 8, Dr. Henry Austin wrote: *I was called to a man who was sick- about 5 A.M. I found him with symptoms of Cholera of which he died at one this day- The train started on the march leaving one wagon in which the sick man was behind. I stayed of course to attend to him the symptoms continue to be less favorable- the train stopped before it proceeded far on this road and returned and layed by for the day- Several of the [men] are preparing for the funeral.*

Captain Bruff described the preparations: *The messmates of the deceased laid him out, sewed him up in his blue blanket, and prepared a bier, formed of his tent-poles. I had a grave dug in a neighboring ridge, on left of the trail, about 400 yards from it. Dry clay and gravel, and coarse white sand-stone on the next hill, afforded slabs to line it with, making a perfect vault (Bruff himself carved the lettering on the head and footstone.) I then organized a funeral procession, men all in clean clothes and uniforms, with music (a key-bugle, flute, violin, and accordion) and two and two, with the Stars & stripes over the body we marched to the measured time of the dirge, deposited the body of our comrade in the grave, an elderly gentleman read the burial service, and we filled up the grave, erected the stones, and returned to camp.*

The funeral was attended by another company, the New York Colony Guards, a military-style company complete with uniforms. They provided a firing party of eight men, giving the ceremony a military air, apparently in honor of Bishop's Mexican War experience. The long-lost grave was rediscovered in 1988 by trail historians William and Jan Hill of Centereach, New York.

Signing and Funding by   OREGON-CALIFORNIA TRAILS ASSOCIATION

1995

This is a part of your American heritage. Honor it, protect it, preserve it for your children.

William Clary Grave

Clary headstone, now lost.
Source unknown.

Randy Brown

General Comments - Long identified as the grave of William L. Clary, the questions of who he was and where he came from have been answered by Graves and Sites Committee research, resulting in the placement of this marker. The fence around the grave was built in 1988 by Randy Brown, Jacques Downs, and Heather Pritchard, all of Douglas, Wyoming. Visitors to this grave are urged to see the nearby graves of Henry Hill and Charles Bishop. All three graves share a common landowner. For more on the Clary grave and neighboring sites,

see "Who Was William Clary?" in the January 1993 issue of *News From the Plains*.

Location - Southeast of Torrington, Goshen County, Wyoming. SE¼SE¼, Sec. 25, T24N, R61W.

Ownership
Gary Nickal
Nickal Brothers Farms
118 Arrowhead Road
Torrington, WY 82240
(307) 532-4770

WILLIAM L. CLARY

Until recently this grave was marked by a headstone that read: Wm. L. CLARY JUNE 21 1850.

On July 3, 1850, Micajah Littleton passed this place and in the evening recorded inscriptions of grave markers he had seen that day. Among nine listed were Geo. A. Gillum, June 21, and Wm. D. Clark also June 21. Littleton may have erred in copying the "Clark" marker, for it is believed that this is indeed the grave of William Clary of Ashley, Pike County, Missouri. Clary died within a few hours of his messmate, George A. Gillum, while they camped with their company on the river below this hill.

Clary and Gillum traveled with a Missouri-to-California cattle drive organized in Pike County by Walter and John Crow. Daniel Clary and his family were neighbors of the Crow clan, and two Clary boys—William, 19, and John, 17—joined the company captained by Walter Crow.

The company was made up of forty-six men mainly from Pike and Lincoln counties in Missouri. They left the contiguous United States west of Independence, Mo., on May 13 with 721 head of loose cattle and sixty-four head of work steers, plus about ten wagons. Apparently William and John Clary were not working for the Crows, as their mess is listed by diarist Cyrus C. Loveland as "a team that traveled with us."

Many of the men were plagued by ill health. On June 10 Levi Armstead of Ashley died near Ash Hollow. On June 15 the Crow company camped on the river near here, and later that evening the Gillum-Clary group came up. They had been left behind on the 13th because of the illness of George Gillum. The next day the main party again went on and left the Gillum-Clary team behind. Left also were two groups from the Crow company to help with the sick, and for at least six days this party remained In camp tending men too ill to travel.

On July 3 the main party camped near Devil's Gate, determined to wait until the balance of the company could catch up. The next day they celebrated Independence Day with a meal of fresh beef and peach pie. Loveland's diary for July 4 reads as follows:

> *This evening we heard from our company behind by the arrival of John Clarey. They have had three deaths since we left them; John Mosier died the 19 June, from Pisgah, Cooper County, Missouri; William Clarey died the 20th June, from Ashley, Pike County Missouri; George Gilam died the 21st June, from Louisville, Lincoln County, Missouri. They all died with the cholera.*

Presumably the graves of John Mosier and George Gillum are close to that of Clary, but only the Clary headstone survived to be recorded by later historians. Although it, too, has now disappeared, its memory allows us to identify, commemorate, and to preserve the grave of William L. Clary, for many years to come.

Researched and placed by the:
Oregon-California Trails Association

1992

This is a part of your American heritage. Honor it, protect it, preserve it for your children.

Leased to
Adam and Teresa Cross
RR2 Box 317A
Torrington, WY 82240
(307) 532-4542

Access - Permission is required to visit the site.

Directions - From the intersection of U.S. 26 and U.S. 85 at Torrington, Wyoming, drive south on U.S. 85 for 2.4 miles. Turn left on Nebraska 92. In 1.3 miles turn left on gravel County Road 126E G5. Drive east 3.8 miles to ranch headquarters to obtain permission and directions to the Clary, Bishop, and Hill graves. This ranch is the home of the leaseholder.

Mary Elizabeth Homsley

Randy Brown

General Comments - During the 1940s, researcher W. W. Morrison of Cheyenne contacted descendants of Mary Homsley in Oregon. The text for this sign is taken from his research, with details added from an interview of Lura Homsley Gibson done in 1932 by Fred Lockley of the *Oregon Journal*. Homsley's interview is in Fred Lockley, *The Lockley Files: Conversations with Pioneer Women,* ed. Mike Helm (Eugene, Ore.: Rainy Day Press, 1981): 173-76.

Location - West of Fort Laramie, Goshen County, Wyoming. SW¼, Sec.17, T26N, R64W.

Directions - From the river bridge between the town of Fort Laramie and Fort Laramie National Historic Site, travel west 0.7 mile and turn right on a county gravel road. In 1.2 miles turn right. The grave is another 0.2 mile north. From the Fort Laramie NHS entrance the road leading to the grave is a left turn in 1 mile. Unless conditions are extremely wet, there is no

need to return to U.S. 26 to reach Guernsey. Leave the Homsley grave site and turn right on the county road. Register Cliff can be reached using this road. The "Bluff" and "Plateau" south-side routes of the Oregon Trail parallel this road for many miles. Look for OCTA's white Carsonite trail markers to the right of the road, then to the left, and back to the right as the trail crosses and recrosses the current road as it heads west. After several miles, watch for Whalen Dam Road. Turn right on it. In about ½ mile down the hill, the Bluff Route crosses this road. Nearer the river, the River Route can be seen crossing Whalen Dam Road. The swales are impressive.

Access - Open to the public.

Ownership
Charles Potter
Fort Laramie, WY 82212
(307) 837-2797

MARY ELIZABETH HOMSLEY

Mary Elizabeth Homsley was born near Lexington, Kentucky, July 20, 1824. She moved with her parents, Jacob and Sarah Oden, to Truxton, Missouri, where she was married to Benjamin Franklin Homsley in 1841. In April 1852, accompanied by Mary's parents and ten brothers and sisters, some with families of their own, they took the trail to Oregon. With Mary and Benjamin went their two little daughters, Lura and Sarah Ellen, but left behind in Missouri were the graves of their two oldest children, twins, who had been poisoned by an embittered slave.

The Homsley company traveled via Council Bluffs. Somewhere in Nebraska Mary gave birth to their fifth child. Before arriving at Fort Laramie Mary and the baby boy were stricken with measles, and the company elected to cross at the fort, perhaps in search of medical aid. The crossing was a disaster. The wagon carrying Mary overturned and she and the baby were thrown into the river. Both were rescued, but Mary's condition worsened that night and on the following day, June 10, she died. She was wrapped in a featherbed and buried here. The baby survived for several weeks, but he, too, passed away when the company was near present Boise, Idaho.

The company went on to Oregon, where Benjamin took a donation land claim on Elliott Prairie, Clackamas County. He raised his two surviving children alone and never remarried. He died in 1908 and is buried in Rock Creek Cemetery in Clackamas County

Mary Homsley's grave was rediscovered in 1925 by passing cowboys. The headstone was enclosed in the present monument the following year. Contacted in Oregon, Lura Homsley Gibson could still vividly recall her mother's death and standing at the lonely grave saying a final good-bye, nearly seventy-five years before.

Research by W. W. Morrison, Cheyenne, Wyo.
Signing and Funding by   **OREGON-CALIFORNIA TRAILS ASSOCIATION**
1991

This is a part of your American heritage. Honor it, protect it, preserve it for your children.

Benjamin Homsley, husband of Mary.

W. W. Morrison Collection
Sarah Ellen Homsley, daughter of Mary.

Warm Springs

Randy Brown

General Comments - One of the most famous Oregon Trail springs is still flowing strongly, just as in trail days. Warm Springs Canyon is in nearly pristine condition, little changed since the covered-wagon era.

Location - Southwest of Guernsey, Platte County, Wyoming. SW¼, Sec. 4, T26N, R66W.

Ownership
Charles Frederick
Guernsey, WY 82214
(307) 836-2456

Access - Permission is required to visit the site. The Frederick family, who owns the property, welcomes responsible visitors but asks that the site be left as it is found. Permission may also be required to cross National Guard property bordering Warm Springs Canyon.

Directions - From the eastern edge of Guernsey, cross the river bridge. Turn left on the first road across the river. Approximately ¾ mile south, turn to the right. Proceed over the hill and then down into a wash, 1 mile. Continue west on a gravel road. Bear to the left at the intersections with dirt roads and proceed about 2 miles to a gate marked: "Private Property. No Motorized Vehicles." The springs are about ¼ mile beyond this gate. Hike from this point. Close the gate when entering and leaving.

WARM SPRINGS

Wagon trains heading west found these springs a convenient one-day's travel twelve miles beyond Fort Laramie. There were two main routes from the fort and emigrants traveling either could utilize this campgound. Though well known to early mountaineers trapping local streams, Warm Springs was first described by John C. Fremont who stopped here on July 21, 1842.

Sometimes called the "Big Springs" by emigrants, Warm Springs is best known in Wyoming folklore as "The Emigrants' Laundry Tub." This later term can be confirmed by at least one account, that of Pusey Graves, who camped nearby on June 24, 1850. He wrote, "After I finished my letter to send back to the Ft. I proceeded to the spring a distance of 1½ miles with my bucket of dirty clothes."

Early settlers found this area littered with wagon train debris and many graves. Of the graves, only one remains to be seen today. It is located across the draw southwest of here.

Research, Signing and Funding by the

OREGON-CALIFORNIA
TRAILS ASSOCIATION

1989

This is a part of your American heritage. Honor it, protect it, preserve it for your children.

Elva Ingram

Randy Brown

James and Ritta Ann (Akin) Ingram,
parents of Elva Ingram.

Jack Ingram

ELVA INGRAM

On April 15, 1852, James and Ritta Ann Ingram, with their nine children, left Salem, Henry County, Iowa, for Pleasant Valley, Oregon. The wagon train, consisting of forty people in four families, reached the Fort Laramie area June 21,1852.

Here on the North Bank (Child's) route, on Wednesday, June 23, 1852, the youngest daughter, Elva Ingram, died, the cause of her death is unknown. She was four years old. On that day eighteen-year-old James Akin, Jr., wrote: "Travel 12 miles very hilly bad roads. pine and cedar bluffs—cloudy rainy weather—Elva Ingram daughter of James and wife died—Camp in good place—Plenty wood no water."

There were seven more deaths in the Richey-Ingram-Akin wagon train, which reached Willamette Valley late in October, 1852.

Research and Signing by

OREGON-CALIFORNIA TRAILS ASSOCIATION

Funded by
Dr. Jack Ingram and family
Medford, Oregon

1987

This is a part of your American heritage. Honor it, protect it, preserve it for your children.

General Comments - Located in the trail era's "Black Hills," specifically on what is known as Emigrant Hill, Elva Ingram's grave is the only one of three graves in the vicinity that can be identified. The authentic-looking headstone may or may not be original. Visitors can view deep trail ruts crossing "the notch" below the grave. In the distance the North Platte River canyons lie far below. It is truly a beautiful place for a historic grave.

Location - Near Hartville, Platte County, Wyoming. NW corner, Sec. 3, T22N, R66W.

Access - Open to the public.

Directions - From Hartville, Wyoming, take the Manville Highway north for about 1 mile. Turn left and follow the road downhill for ¾ mile to the foot of Emigrant Hill. Continue straight ahead up the winding road climbing Emigrant Hill. Turn left ¼ mile after reaching the top. The Ingram grave is in the pasture to the left, ¼ mile after turning.

Mily/Millie Irwin

Reg Duffin

about two miles south of the Irwin grave. Many miles west the company, captained by Robert Irwin, turned south off the main Oregon Trail and took the Applegate Trail or "Southern Route" into Oregon.

There are seven identified graves of emigrants in Wyoming who died during the "cholera year" of 1852 when it is estimated that 5,000 individuals died on the trail. All are marked, or were until fairly recently, by large sandstone headstones. The Mily Irwin headstone can be seen at the Glendo Museum. The exact site of the grave, once marked by a steel post, is in an alfalfa field about fifty feet west of the OCTA marker.

The grave site area was fenced and marked in 1998 by Randy Brown. Two of Brown's students, Kassidy and Gena Falkenburg assisted in the fence construction.

Location - Approximately eight miles south of Glendo, Wyoming.

Directions - Please contact OCTA member Nancy Curtis, daughter of Bill Johnson, for permission to visit and to obtain the best current directions to the grave site.

Access - Permission is required to visit the site.

Ownership
William H. Johnson
403 Cassa Road
Glendo, WY 82213
(307) 735-4354

Nancy Curtis
P.O. Box 123
Glendo, WY 82213
(307) 735-4370

General Comments - The Grave of Mily, or Millie, Irwin is located on the North Platte River near old Cassa, Wyoming. The grave site is a half mile from the trail and is on what must have been a campground for wagon trains using the "River Route" branch of the Oregon Trail. The River Route begins near Warm Springs, approximately fourteen miles west of Fort Laramie. The trail crosses the high divide between Horseshoe and "Bitter" Cottonwood Creek and descends via a steep hill into Horseshoe Creek Valley

MILLIE IRWIN

On May 19, 1852, the *St. Joseph Gazette* carried an item describing the year's large overland emigration. It noted that many residents of St. Joseph, Missouri, were already on their way to California. "Many of our leading citizens to whom we were strongly attached have left within the last ten days and are now wending their way across the plains. Among the emigrants from the city and immediate neighborhood, we would mention the names of Judge Irwin and family."

Judge Irwin, 53, was Tennessee-born Robert Irwin, a justice of the peace in Buchanan County. Instead of going to California, Irwin and family were heading for Oregon. With them was his wife Millie, 55, a native of North Carolina. Robert had traveled over the plains to Oregon in 1850 with their second son, Francis, to look the land over. Robert had met with his approval, so now he and Millie were moving there with their entire family: youngest son William, age 18; oldest son James and his wife, Rebecca, with their five-year old son Samuel; and only daughter, the widow Sylvina Irwin Means, with her four children—fifteen-year old Nancy, George, who was eleven, Susan, seven, and five-year old Martha Ann. Francis Irwin had remained in Oregon.

On June 10, 1852, at a campground near here on the North Platte River, Millie Irwin died. This is the site of her grave. According to the recollection of her granddaughter Susan, the cause of death was cholera.

The Irwin family suffered other losses. Sylvina Irwin Means died near present Imlay, Nevada, of mountain fever. An emigrant copied the inscription on her grave marker: "Mrs. Salvina [sic] Means, died August 13, 1852. age 32 years." A few days later George Means died. Thus Robert Irwin left his wife, a daughter, and a grandson, all in graves on the trail to Oregon.

Robert Irwin and the surviving members of his family settled near Philomath, Benton County, Oregon. He married again to Grace "Nannie" (Jasper) Langston on May 1, 1853. Nannie and her husband John Langston had crossed the plains with Robert and Francis Irwin in 1850, but John Langston did not survive the journey. Together, Robert and Nannie Irwin raised the orphaned Means children. According to Susan Means, Robert later had "charge of Columbia College in Eugene, Oregon, where the children attended school for three years." Robert Irwin died on July 13, 1876, at Beaver Creek, Benton County, Oregon. He was 77.

This grave was discovered around 1985 by landowner Bill Johnson. The inscription on the headstone, a sandstone slab now in the Glendo Museum is lightly etched but clearly legible:

MilY. IRWiN
died June THE 10
1852
A. 55. y. MO

Research, Signing, and Funding by:

THE OREGON-CALIFORNIA TRAILS ASSOCIATION

1998

This is a part of your American heritage. Honor it, protect it, preserve it for your children.

McKinstry Ridge

Randy Brown

General Comments - During the years 1948 to 1973, Viola McKinstry accompanied her husband Bruce L. McKinstry on most of the twenty-four western trips he made to explore, locate, and follow the exact route taken by his grandfather Byron McKinstry in 1850. Mrs. McKinstry, who knows this remote trail area of Wyoming so well, treasures the knowledge that the ridge now carries the name honoring her husband's efforts as well as Byron McKinstry's 1850 overland journey.

Location - North of Douglas, Converse County, Wyoming. SW¼, Sec. 9, T33N, R71W.

Ownership
Bridget Paich
201 Combs Rd.
Douglas, WY 82633
 (307) 358-2649

Access - Permission of the owner is required to visit the site.

Permission must also be granted by a neighboring landowner, whose land is crossed to reach McKinstry Ridge. Write or call:
    Bob Hageman
    280 Highway 59
    Douglas, WY 82133
    (307) 358-3850

Directions - Access is to four-wheel drive vehicles only!

Leave Douglas on Wyoming 59. About 1 mile north, turn left on Airport Road. In 0.7 mile, turn right on gravel road. Continue 1.3 miles to a windmill and gate. Proceed through the gate, leaving it closed or open, as you find it. (It will probably be closed but, if you find it open, leave

McKINSTRY RIDGE

On June 26,1850, portions of two emigrant companies, the Upper Mississippi Ox Company and the Wisconsin Blues, passed this way en route to the gold fields of California. They are believed to be the first wagon trains to follow a route beyond Fort Laramie that remained north of the N. Platte River. This trail segment, ending at the ferries of the Platte at present-day Glenrock and Casper, is known as Child's Cutoff, named for Andrew Child of Waukesha, Wisconsin, whose emigrant guidebook was published in 1852.

School teacher Byron N. McKinstry of McHenry County, Illinois, was, like Andrew Child, a member of the Upper Mississippi Ox Company. His diary entry for June 26 describes this stretch of the trail:

"After following the river for 5 or 6 m. we crossed some very rough ground. Following a kind of divide first rising in a Northerly direction to the summit, then turning S.W. and descending to the Platte,—the crookedest road possible. These hills are bare and have a wild savage appearance, but little vegetation on them. Camped on the Platte. Poor grass. 20 m."

McKinstry's diary, published in 1975 and edited by his grandson, Bruce L. McKinstry, has become a classic trail account. This stretch of Child's Cutoff, described so vividly by Byron, is named McKinstry Ridge in his honor and also for grandson Bruce, who, by tracing his grandfather's journey across the country, has made an invaluable contribution to trail scholarship.

Research, Signing and Funding by the:

OREGON-CALIFORNIA TRAILS ASSOCIATION

Funding by:
Mrs. Viola McKinstry
Riverside, Illinois

1988

This is a part of your American heritage. Honor it, protect it, preserve it for your children.

it open.) Continue straight ahead 0.6 mile to where the trail crosses left to right. Deep ruts are visible here. Follow the road, which turns north. Follow winding road 0.6 mile to a second gate, reached after a sharp left turn. Pass through the gate, leaving it closed or open, as you find it. Immediately turn right, up a hill along the fence line. This begins McKinstry Ridge. Follow the road, essentially on the trail, up and down washes 1.4 miles to the marker. Return the way you came or continue north 0.5 mile. Turn left and follow a ranch road and trail about 2 miles to the river. From where you reach the river, it is 1¾ miles to a fence and gate. Pass through the gate and go left around a corn field. It is about 3 miles to paved Ross Road. Turn left to return to Douglas.

Joel Hembree and Ralston Baker Grave Sites

Reg Duffin

General Comments - For more information on the Joel Hembree grave, see Reg Duffin, "The Grave of Joel Hembree," *Overland Journal* 3, no. 2 (Spring 1985): 6-16.

Location - West of Douglas, Converse County, Wyoming. NW¼, Sec. 15, T32N, R73W.

Ownership
 Leroy "Butch" and Jodie White
274 Natural Bridge Rd.
Douglas, WY 82633
(307) 358-2082

Access - Permission is required to visit the site.

Directions - From I-25 turn off at Exit 151. Drive 3 miles south to the Natural Bridge Ranch, where you will find the land owners. Ask for permission and directions at the ranch.

JOEL HEMBREE

Joel Jordan Hembree, his wife Sara (Sally) and their eight sons from McMinnville, Tennessee, were part of the estimated 1,000 men, women and children who left Fitzhugh's Mill near Independence, Missouri, in May 1843, for Oregon.

On July 18, between Bed Tick Creek and here at La Prele Creek, six-year-old Joel Hembree, the second youngest son, fell from the wagon tongue on which he was riding and was fatally injured.

Diarist William T. Newby wrote, July 18: "A very bad road. Joel J. Hembrees son Joel fel off the waggeon tung & both wheels run over him. Distance 17 miles." July 19: "Lay buy. Joel Hembree departed this life about 2 o'clock." July 20: "We buried the youth & ingraved his name on the headstone." Dr. Marcus Whitman described the fatality as "a wagon having passed over the abdomen." This is the oldest identified grave along the Oregon Trail.

Joel's body, originally buried ¼ mile east, was moved here March 24, 1962, and placed beside Pvt. Ralston Baker, who was killed in an Indian skirmish on May 1, 1867.

North 400 feet is the site of the 1860s La Prele Stage and Pony Express station.

Research and Signing by

OREGON-CALIFORNIA TRAILS ASSOCIATION

Fencing and Sign Funding by the

PAUL C. HENDERSON
MEMORIAL FUND

1987

This is a part of your American heritage. Honor it, protect it, preserve it for your children.

Mary J. Hurley [Kelly] Grave

Randy Brown

General Comments - This grave has traditionally been known as the Mary Kelly grave. Recent research by Randy Brown has established that Mary Hurley Kelly was the niece and possibly adopted daughter of Josiah and Fanny Kelly.

For more information, see Randy Brown, "Attack on the Kelly-Larimer Wagon Trail," *Overland Journal* 5, no. 1 (Winter 1987): 16-40.

Location - About 14 miles west of Douglas, Converse County, Wyoming. SE¼, Sec. 35, T33N, R74W.

Ownership
Bill and Edna Barber
71 Barber Road
Douglas, WY 82633
(307) 358-2658

Access - Permission is required to visit site.

Directions - From I-25 take the Barber Exit south to the Barber Ranch. Request permission to visit the grave site at the ranch house.

MARY J. HURLEY

On July 12, 1864, a small Montana-bound wagon train was attacked by Sioux Indians a half-mile east at Little Box Elder crossing. The four men buried here were killed immediately: Noah Taylor of Coffey County, Kansas; Mr. Sharp, a Methodist minister probably from Wilson Co., Kansas; one unknown; and Franklin, sixteen-year-old Negro servant of Josiah and Fanny Kelly.

The Kellys, from Allen, Co., Kansas, were accompanied by their niece, seven-year-old Mary J. Hurley. Fanny and Mary, with Sarah Larimer, and son, were taken captive. Mary escaped that night and found her way back to the trail near here but was overtaken and killed just as she was about to be rescued by passing soldiers. Her body was discovered and buried here a few days later.

These graves were identified and restored in 1946 by W. W. Morrison of Cheyenne. When the dam across Little Box Elder was built in 1954, the remains of the four men were removed from their original burial place in the valley and reinterred beside the grave of Mary Hurley.

Research and signing by the:

OREGON-CALIFORNIA
TRAILS ASSOCIATION

1988

This is a part of your American heritage. Honor it, protect it, preserve it for your children.

1954 dedication at restored graves of Mary Kelly and the four men killed by Indians. L. C. Bishop at left, and W. W. Morrison with microphone.

W. W. Morrison Collection

Alvah H. Unthank Grave

Randy Brown

Location - East of Glenrock, Converse County, Wyoming. SW¼SW¼, Sec. 18, T33N, R74W.

Access - None! The temptation will be to climb through the wire fence for a close view of the Unthank grave. Please do not do this. The owner, having experienced vandalism on his property, emphatically forbids trespassing. This is his right.

Directions to Marker - Approximately 5 miles ESE of Glenrock, opposite the Dave Johnson Power Plant.

At the Glenrock East exit from I-25, turn north on County Road 27. The grave is on the right, approximately ½ mile from the turnoff, near a small parking area along the road.

Do not cross the fence onto the private property.

ALVAH H. UNTHANK

Nineteen-year-old Alvah Unthank was one of a group of young men who left Newport, Wayne County, Indiana, for the goldfields of California in 1850. On June 23 the wagon train passed Register Cliff, south of Guernsey. There Alvah inscribed his name: A. H. UNTHANK 1850.

In the early evening hours of June 28 the party made camp here by the North Platte River on account of the sudden sickness of Alvah. On June 29 a family friend, Pusey Graves, wrote: "Lay by today to doctor and nurse Alvah. June 30 Alvah getting worse it's quite hopeless complaining none. July 1 Alvah is rapidly sinking. July 2 in the early morning hours Alvah died." Cholera had taken its toll.

Graves wrote: "Alvah lay calm, bore his suffering patiently and uttered not a murmur or groan. Bid his father to be of good cheer. His child has paid the great debt of nature. Procured a large neat headstone." Solomon Woody carved the inscription. At noon Tuesday, July 2, 1850, the solemn task of burial took place.

Research, Signing and Funding by   1987

OREGON-CALIFORNIA TRAILS ASSOCIATION

This is a part of your American heritage. Honor it, protect it, preserve it for your children.

Markers near the Alvah H. Unthank site.

Randy Brown

Martin Ringo and J. P. Parker Gravesites

Randy Brown

General Comments - The graves of Martin Ringo and J. P. Parker are protected by iron-pipe fencing erected about 1930 by Troop 81 of the Boy Scouts of America, Casper, Wyoming.

Recently available diaries enabled Randy Brown to summarize the sad circumstances of Martin Ringo's death for the OCTA marker text. The marker was dedicated Friday, July 14th, 1987, with OCTA Director Mary Mueller of San Jose, California, giving a talk on the Ringo family.

Another steel marker erected by OCTA's Graves and Site Committee in 1986 marks the Ringo gravesite, with the text: "Mexican War veteran Martin Ringo was accidently shot near this spot on July 29, 1864. Widow and five children continued on to San Jose, Calif."

For more information, refer to Randy Brown, "The Death of Martin Ringo," *Overland Journal* 7, no. 1 (1989): 20-23.

Location - Two miles west of Glenrock, Converse County, Wyoming. NW¼, Sec. 1, T33N, R76W.

Ownership
W. L. Miles
805 HW 20-26
Glenrock, WY 82637

Access - Permission is required to visit the site.

Directions - From the west edge of Glenrock, drive west on U.S. 26 for approximately 2 miles to a gate on the north side of the road. Ask permission to visit the grave at the house within the fence line.

MARTIN RINGO

On May 18, 1864, Martin and Mary Peters Ringo left their home in Gallatin, Missouri, intending to settle in California. With them went their five children, John, Albert, Fanny, Enna, and Mattie.

The wagon train they traveled with - some seventy wagons grouped together for mutual protection - camped here on the night of July 29. Early the next morning, as Ringo climbed up his wagon, his shotgun went off in his own hands, killing him instantly. He was forty-five years old.

A friend, William Davenport, wrote: "He was buried near the place he was shot, in as decent a manner as was possible with the facilities on the plains."

The family eventually reached San Jose, California, the home of Coleman and Augusta Younger, brother-in-law and sister of Mary Ringo. Mary Enna Ringo, daughter of Martin and Mary Ringo, became an outstanding teacher in the San Jose school system for over fifty years.

Buried next to Ringo is J. P. Parker. Parker's tombstone tells all that is known of his life and death.

Research and Signing by

OREGON-CALIFORNIA TRAILS ASSOCIATION

Funding by
SAN JOSE ADULT EDUCATION
ARGONAUTS
IN MEMORY OF FERNE V. GALE

1987

This is a part of your American heritage. Honor it, protect it, preserve it for your children.

Ada Magill

Randy Brown

General Comments - The grave of this three-year-old child has been a survivor. Moved in 1912 to avoid highway construction, a railway spur line now runs close to the head of the grave. But little Ada remains safe and secure her grave, well marked by a 1912 Oregon Trail marker, a Pony Express marker, and an interpretive marker placed by OCTA in July 1987.

Location - Five miles west of Glenrock, Converse County, Wyoming. SW¼, Sec. 3, T33N, R76W.

Ownership - Converse County, Wyoming. (County road right-of-way.)

Access - Open to the public.

Directions - Approximately 2.7 miles west of the Ringo-Parker site (page 50), turn north on gravel road. In 0.1 mile, turn west. The grave is about 100 yards down this road.

ADA MAGILL

Caleb and Nancy Magill with their six children were part of a wagon train traveling from Brown County, Kansas, to Dallas, Oregon, in 1864. After leaving Fort Laramie their three-year old daughter Ada was taken sick with dysentery. At Deer Creek Station she worsened. An hour before dawn on July 3, 1864, Ada died. In "Sunday best tiny calico dress" she was buried on a small rise of ground just south of here.

In 1912 a new highway under construction was to have passed directly over Ada's grave. Her remains were moved thirty feet north to this spot. Wyoming's state engineer, Loren Clark Bishop, fashioned the headstone which now marks the final resting place of this pioneer child.

The Oregon Trail is about fifty feet south of this spot.

Research, Signing and Funding by

OREGON-CALIFORNIA TRAILS ASSOCIATION   1987

 This is a part of your American heritage. Honor it, protect it, preserve it for your children.

Caleb W. Magill, father of Ada Magill. He worked as a teamster, freighting supplies to Fort Laramie before the family went to Oregon.

W. W. Morrison Collection

Quintina Snodderly

Randy Brown

Jacob Snodderly, husband of Quintina.

Courtesy of Max Barzee

General Comments - Quintina (Latin, meaning "fifth born") Arminda Lett was the daughter of Francis C. Lett and Elizabeth Thompson who were married September 21, 1797, in Mecklenburg County, Virginia. Quintina married Jacob Snodderly circa 1829 in Knox County, Tennessee. They had nine children. The grave was discovered in summer 1974 during road construction. Landowners Bill and Kathy Fritts identified the remains as Quintina Snodderly's and wrote the text of the sign. No written accounts in family papers describe the circumstances or cause of her death. A more recent assessment of the skeletal remains did not reveal any evidence of trauma.

Following the discovery of the grave, archaeologists removed Quintina Snodderly's remains for extensive examination. After the examination was completed, OCTA helped finance a pine coffin, and the remains of Quintina Snodderly were finally laid to rest here on June 16, 1988, by Jim Rankin, Jacque Downs, and Randy Brown.

QUINTINA SNODDERLY

A pioneer mother, Quintina Snodderly, died near here on June 25, 1852. A native of Tennessee, Quintina, with her husband, Jacob, and their eight children (five girls and three boys) had lived in Clarinda County, Iowa, for several years before embarking on their trip across the plains. They were members of a wagon train captained by Rev. Joab Powell, which had left St. Joseph, Missouri, in the spring of 1852.

Quintina's grave was discovered and excavated in 1974. An examination of the skeleton revealed the cause of death. Most of the ribs had been crushed, probably by the heavy wheels of a covered wagon. The skeleton was in otherwise perfect condition, with fragments of a green ribbon bow still around the neck. The Powell wagon train probably crossed the North Platte River at this point and the accident may have occurred as the wagons climbed the river bluffs to enter the north bank trail.

Jacob and the children reached Linn County, Oregon, and several descendants still reside in that area.

The grave was restored and fence constructed here in 1987, by the Oregon-California Trails Association. It is a few feet from the original site.

Research and Signing by
KATHERINE & BILL FRITTS and the

OREGON-CALIFORNIA TRAILS ASSOCIATION

Funding by

NATRONA COUNTY
HISTORICAL SOCIETY

1987

This is a part of your American heritage. Honor it, protect it, preserve it for your children.

For more information, see Randy Brown, "The Grave of Quintina Snodderly," *Overland Journal* 7, no. 1 (1989): 23-25.

Location - West of Glenrock, Natrona County, Wyoming. S½, Sec. 32, T34N, R77W.

Ownership
Dennis and Brenda Ford
12333 Geary Dome Rd. (Co. Rd. 704)
Evansville, WY 82636
(307) 789-5616

Access - Permission is required to visit the site.

Directions - From the Magill grave (page 52), go about 5 miles west on U.S. 87/U.S. 20/26,

turn north onto County Road 21 (Coal Shadow Road). Proceed about 1 mile across the river and railroad tracks. Turn west on an unnamed county road and proceed 3.2 miles to a gate on the left.

From Casper, proceed east on U.S. 87/U.S. 20/26, 2.9 miles to County Road 256 (Cole Creek Road), or exit I-25 on Hat Six Road. Turn north and cross the river. Continue 2.5 miles to Geary Dome Road. Turn east and proceed 5 miles to a gate on the right.

Drive through the gate and proceed 0.3 mile to the bottom of the hill and ask permission to visit the grave at the log house located there.

Richard's Bridge Marker

RESHAW'S BRIDGE
1852-65

Thousands of emigrants following the Oregon-California Trail crossed the North Platte River over a bridge built here by John Richard (Reshaw). The $5 toll during high water saved swimming or ferrying across, and saved countless lives in the process.

Fort Clay, also known as Camp Davis, was established here in 1855 to protect the bridge. Camp Payne was also located here in 1858-59.

Research and Signing by

**OREGON-CALIFORNIA
TRAILS ASSOCIATION**

Funding by

WYOMING STATE
HISTORICAL SOCIETY

1987

 This is a part of your American heritage. Honor it, protect it, preserve it for your children.

General Comments - In 1853 John Richard Sr. built a toll bridge to replace the earlier ferries in the vicinity of Casper, where south-side emigrants crossed the North Platte River. Since Richard was of French descent, his name was pronounced and usually written as Reshaw.

In 1859 another bridge was built six miles upstream, at the later site of Fort Caspar, and north-side travelers began crossing Richard's Bridge to avoid the sandhills on the old road, crossing again on the upper bridge.

A sizeable community developed on the south side of Richard's Bridge, including a store, blacksmith shop, and occasional military posts.

Location - Evansville, Natrona County, Wyoming. NE¼SW¼, Sec. 36, T34N, R79W.

Ownership - Town of Evansville, Wyoming.

Access - Open to the public.

Directions - In Evansville, on the eastern edge of Casper, go north on Oregon Trail National Cemetery Road, turn left at the river's edge into Evansville Town Park.

The Oregon-California Trail Marker

THE OREGON-CALIFORNIA TRAIL

During the years 1841 to 1867 over 350,000 persons passed through Casper on their way west. The majority of them traveled through what is now the lobby of the First Interstate Bank. The promise of free land, sudden riches, or religious freedom caused these pioneers to endure the great hardships of a very difficult trail. Thousands of persons died in the quest and are buried along the old highway. This was the largest overland migration in history.

Research and Signing by

OREGON-CALIFORNIA TRAILS ASSOCIATION

Funding by

First Interstate Bank of Casper

1987

 This is a part of your American heritage. Honor it, protect it, preserve it for your children.

General Comments - In cooperation with the Natrona County Historical Society, OCTA placed an Oregon-California Trail marker in the First Interstate Bank outdoor plaza in downtown Casper, Wyoming. The marker was dedicated during OCTA's 1987 convention that was held in Casper.

Location - First Interstate Outdoor Plaza, downtown Casper, Wyoming.

Ownership - First Interstate Bank of Casper.

Access - Open to the public.

Directions - The Plaza is at the intersection of 1st and Center in downtown Casper, Wyoming. (Refer to a Casper street map.)

Frederick Richard Fulkerson

Randy Brown

General Comments - This grave site has long been identified as the final resting place of T. P. Baker. The OCTA marker corrects that misunderstanding. Information on the Fulkerson family was gathered by Frances Milne of Pullman, Washington. Details concerning the identification of the Fulkerson grave is in the October 1993 issue of the *News From the Plains*. Richard Smith of Casper built and donated the steel fence around the Fulkerson grave, and it was installed at the grave site by a group of OCTA Wyoming Chapter members in 1996.

Location - Near Devil's Gate, Natrona County, Wyoming. NW¼, Sec. 36, T29N, R87W.

Directions - From the Devil's Gate visitor center, head east on the old highway to Rattlesnake Pass. The grave is on the south side of this road. Look for the steel fence and wooden cross.

Access - Open to the public.

Ownership - State of Wyoming.

FREDERICK RICHARD FULKERSON

The grave of F. R. Fulkerson was noted by forty-niner J. G. Bruff on July 26, 1849, as he traveled through what he termed "Pass of the Rattle-Snake Mountain to the left of Devil's Gate." The survival of the large granite boulder used as the Fulkerson headstone and the sketch made of it by Bruff allows us to locate this grave precisely.

Frederick Richard Fulkerson, son of James M. and Mary Fulkerson, died July 1, 1847 while en route to Oregon. His father, James Monroe Fulkerson, was born in Lee County, Virginia, August 28, 1802. The family moved west to Tennessee in 1807 and then on to the Missouri frontier in 1817, where they settled in present Cole County. In 1823 James married Virginia-born Mary Ramsey Miller. By 1847 they had seven children. Frederick, their fourth child and oldest son, was born October 11, 1829.

In the spring of 1847 the Fulkersons and many of their relatives became part of an Oregon-bound party composed primarily of members of the Old Florence Baptist Church located near Jefferson City. Some three hundred congregation members joined a wagon train captained by James Curl. The 120-wagon company soon broke into four groups. The group calling itself "The Plains Baptist Church" was captained by the Reverend Richard Miller, who was Mary Fulkerson's brother and the husband of Nancy Leeper Fulkerson, a sister of James Fulkerson.

Accounts of the death of Frederick Fulkerson vary. The Curl family remembered it thus: *"Mrs. [Caleb] Curl's [née Margaret Fulkerson] brother took the fever, and Mr. Fulkerson, with two other families remained while the others went on. After nine days the young man, then aged eighteen, died near Devil's Gate."* A granddaughter of James and Mary wrote: *"When crossing the Platte River [Frederick] swam the river below the crossing to ford the stock over, as the river was so swift it tended to wash them downstream. He became so chilled and exhausted that he died and was buried near the crossing."*

When Bruff passed the grave in 1849 he also noted, "Inscribed on a rock above the grave 'J.M. Fulkerson, June 26 '47.'" The inscription, which no longer exists, confirms that the family must have camped for at least a week during the final illness of Frederick Fulkerson. Upon his death a grave was dug at the foot of this rock. According to Bruff, the epitaph was painted on the face of the rock headstone, FREDERIC RICHARD, SON OF JAMES M. & MARY FULKERSON, DIED JULY 1, 1847. AGED 18 Years.

Two weeks later Mary Fulkerson died of mountain fever and was buried atop Names Hill on the Green River crossing of the Sublette Cutoff. Bruff saw this grave on August 7, 1849, and noted the engraving on a sandstone slab above the grave: *Mary consort of J.M. Fulkerson. Died July 14, 1847.* The site of Mary Fulkerson's grave became a burial ground for other victims of the trail and eventually developed into a pioneer cemetery. All these graves were destroyed by pipeline construction in the 1930s.

The existing inscription, T. P. Baker 1864, now found on the Frederick Fulkerson gravestone, is believed to be the graffiti of a passing traveler. Baker, whoever he was, left another nearly identical inscription on a rock face a half-mile farther on at the bank of the river.

Signing and Funding by

OREGON-CALIFORNIA TRAILS ASSOCIATION

1995

This is a part of your American heritage. Honor it, protect it, preserve it for your children.

Bennett Tribbett Grave

Randy Brown

Tribbett, drawn from tintype.

Tribbett headboard at the Fort Caspar Museum.

General Information - Renowned Western photographer and artist William Henry Jackson photographed the Bennett Tribbett grave in summer 1870. Some published reproductions of this photo clearly show a wooden board grave marker with distinct lettering: "B T KILLED BY INDIANS," and it has been generally accepted that Tribbet died as a result of Indian action in April 1862. It is now believed that these prints have been altered, perhaps in an effort to sensationalize the photo. The original Tribbett grave marker is now a part of the collections of the Fort Caspar Museum. The inscription, still clearly legible, reads:

"BENNET TRIBBETT
A PRIVATE OF CO
B
11th OHIO CAV
DIED
Dec. 12. 1862.
AGE 22 YRS

(The designation "11th Ohio" indicates that the marker was placed many months after Tribbett's death, since the 11th Ohio was not organized until July 1863.) A foot board inscribed "B T" has also survived. Furthermore, in 1984 the Lander office of the BLM received from a Tribbett family member a letter describing the death of Bennett Tribbett, which is the source for the information on this marker. The letter, along with a badly deteriorated tintype photograph of Tribbett, were subsequently donated to the Fort Caspar Museum.

Ownership - Western Nuclear Corporation.

Leased by
Jack Corbett
1090 Graham Road
Lander, WY 82520
(307) 544-2357

BENNETT TRIBBETT

Private Bennett Tribbett was a nineteen-year-old soldier stationed here at Three Crossings Station. He was a member of Company B of the First Battalion, Sixth Ohio Volunteer Cavalry. On December 14, 1862, Tribbett died of appendicitis. His burial was described by Pvt. Anthony Barleon in a letter written to Bennett's sister, Arviley, at home in Athens County, Ohio.

"We made a coffin of such lumber that we had which of course were rough boards but we planed them off as smooth as we could. We dressed him up in his best clothes which were new and clean, laid a blanket around him, and we tucked a blanket around the coffin which made it look a little better...When the time arrived for his burial he was bore off by the arms of 6 of his former associates accompanied by an escort of six men who performed the usual military escort and ceremony. When we arrived at the grave we put the coffin in and the escort fired three rounds over his grave. So he was buried with all the military honors of a soldier."

In July 1863, four newly recruited companies were consolidated with the old battalion to form a new regiment, designated the Eleventh Ohio Volunteer Cavalry, which continued to serve on the frontier until the last companies were mustered out on July 14, 1866. By Civil War standards, casualties in this regiment were light. Three officers and fifteen men died as a result of actions against Indians; one officer and fifty-eight men, like Bennett Tribbett, died of natural causes.

Research, Signing and Funding by the

OREGON-CALIFORNIA TRAILS ASSOCIATION

1988

 This is a part of your American heritage. Honor it, protect it, preserve it for your children.

William Henry Jackson photo of Tribbett grave at Three Crossings of the Sweetwater River, 1870. S. R. Gifford, an artist with the U. S. Geological Survey, inspects the Tribbett grave marker.

American Heritage Center, University of Wyoming / U.S.G.S.

Location - Six miles east of Jeffrey City, Fremont County, Wyoming. NW¼ SW¼, Sec. 4, T29N, R91W.

Access - Permission is required to visit the site; you must ask for updates on latest directions.

Directions - Obtain permission and directions for the best route to the grave from the lease-holder. Conditions at certain times of the year may make a visit to the grave site impossible.

Parting of the Ways Monument

Randy Brown

Left fork goes to Fort Bridger, right fork is the Sublette Cutoff. Pictured are Troy Gray and Rudy Chesnovar.

General Comments - Perhaps among the first facts a serious student of the overland trails learns is that the Parting of the Ways monument located at the Wyoming 28 parking area west of South Pass is incorrect. The actual Parting of the Ways was not at that site, despite what the monument indicates. However, even though it is incorrect, the marker has now become an accepted part of trail lore and is simply referred to as the "False Parting of the Ways" monument. OCTA's marker is intended to correct the error on the monument and direct the traveler to the actual site.

Location - About 15 miles east of Farson, Sweetwater County, Wyoming. NW¼SW¼, Sec. 25, T27N, R103W.

Ownership - State of Wyoming.

Access - Open to the Public.

Directions - Parking area on the north side of Wyoming 28, 24 miles northeast of Farson.

THE PARTING OF THE WAYS

In July 1844 the California bound Stevens-Townsend-Murphy wagon train, guided by Isaac Hitchcock and 81-year old Caleb Greenwood, passed this point and continued nine and one half miles west southwest from here, to a place destined to become prominent in Oregon Trail history—the starting point of the Sublette Cutoff.

There, instead of following the regular Oregon Trail route southwest to Fort Bridger, then northwest to reach the Bear river below present day Cokeville, Wyoming, this wagon train pioneered a new route. Either Hitchcock or Greenwood, it is uncertain which, made the decision to lead the wagons due west, in effect along one side of a triangle.

The route was hazardous, entailing crossing some 50 miles of semi-arid desert in the heat of summer and surmounting mountain ridges, but it saved approximately 48 miles from the Fort Bridger route and 5 or 6 days travel. The route was first known as the Greenwood Cutoff.

It was the Gold Rush year of 1849 that brought this "Parting of the Ways" into prominence. Of the estimated 30,000 Forty-niners probably 20,000 travelled the Greenwood Cutoff which, due to an error in the 1849 Joseph E. Ware guide book, became known as the Sublette Cutoff.

In the ensuing years further refinements of the trail route were made. In 1852 the Kinney and Slate Creek Cutoffs diverted trains from portions of the Sublette Cutoff, but until the covered wagon period ended, the Sublette Cutoff remained a popular direct route, and this "Parting of the Ways" was the place for crucial decisions.

A quartzite post inscribed ← Fort Bridger   S. Cutoff → and a Bureau of Land Management information panel now mark the historic "Parting of the Ways" site.

Research and signing by the: **OREGON-CALIFORNIA**   1988
TRAILS ASSOCIATION

This is a part of your American heritage. Honor it, protect it, preserve it for your children.

David Bond - died 1864.
Lander Road near
Piney Creek, Wyoming.

Wm. Durham - died July 18, 1859.
I. M. Mead - died July 1, 1864.
Lander Road, Snyder Basin,
Wyoming.

J. W. Lane - died 1859.
Lander Road,
Lane's Creek, Idaho.

Randy Brown

Charles Hatch Grave

Randy Brown

General Comments - The meager details inscribed on the headstone, "IN MEMORY OF CHARLES HATCH   40   DIED JUNE 12 1850," and "Killed by Indians" scratched in lightly to the right of the top line, is all that is known about the life and death of pioneer Charles Hatch.

Location - Two miles southwest of Farson, Sweetwater County, Wyoming. NW¼, Sec. 6, R106W.

Ownership
Marvin Applequist
Box 55
Farson, WY 82932
(307) 273-9311

Access - Permission is required to visit the site. Permission is readily given.

Directions - Drive approximately 2 miles southwest from Farson on the Fontenelle Highway. The Hatch grave is approximately 200 yards south of the highway.

Daniel Lantz

Randy Brown

General Comments - Randy Brown recently identified this grave using partial descriptions of the original headstone, which is now illegible, and diaries kept by Daniel Lantz's companions. Lee Underbrink and Randy Brown constructed the fence and erected the marker in June 1990. See Randy Brown, "Daniel Lantz and the Wayne County Companies of 1850," *Overland Journal* 9, no. 3 (Fall 1991): 2-13.

Location - Three and a half miles northeast of Granger, Sweetwater County, Wyoming. SE¼, Sec. 14, T19N, R111W.

Ownership - Public land, Bureau of Land Management.

Access - Open to the public.

Directions - From Granger, turn west on U.S. 30. Proceed under the railroad overpass and in about ¼ mile, turn north on a gravel road. The grave is on the right, about 3 miles northeast.

DANIEL LANTZ

On April 2,1850, a California-bound company of gold seekers left their homes in the Wayne County, Indiana, towns of Richmond, Boston, and Centerville. Daniel Lantz, age 45, a wagon maker from Centerville, was a member of this party.

The company arrived here at Black's Fork on July 9. Daniel Lantz had been ill for several days, but on July 10 his condition was so much worse that the company agreed to stop "until there was a change in him for better or worse." They camped all that day and the next. The dying man was tended by the company's doctor, Dr. David S. Evans of Boston, who did not believe that Lantz could live another morning.

James Seaton of Centerville recorded the death of Daniel Lantz in his diary entry for July 12, 1850: "Mr. Lantz is still alive but insensible. He lived until 9½ o'clock A.M. When he was no more he was buried at sunset near the road in a very decent manner. His grave was marked by a neat stone. His disease was the bloody flux. There are 10 more get the same disease but none serious."

Daniel Lantz left a wife, Mary, and five children behind in Indiana to mourn their loss. The Centerville company reached Johnson's Ranch near Hangtown in the California goldfields on September 15.

Research, Signing and Funding by the

**OREGON-CALIFORNIA
TRAILS ASSOCIATION**

1989

This is a part of your American heritage. Honor it, protect it, preserve it for your children.

Lucinda B. Wright Grave

Randy Brown

General Comments - Long one of the great mysteries of the trail, the identity of this grave's occupant was determined by the research of Reg and Dorothy Duffin. Reg was OCTA's first Graves and Sites Committee chairman. The complete story can be found in the spring 1998 issue of *Annals of Wyoming*. The grave site is in a remote location on the Green River Desert segment of the Sublette Cutoff. A four-wheel drive vehicle, dry roads, and extreme caution are required for visitation.

The grave was fenced and marked in summer 1998 by Randy Brown.

Location - Approximately fifteen miles east of Names Hill and La Barge, Wyoming.

Ownership - Public lands, Bureau of Land Management.

Access - Open to the public.

LUCINDA B. WRIGHT

Lucinda B. Wright was born in the fall of 1806 in a settlement on Drakes Fork, a tributary of the Green River, in south-central Kentucky. She was the eldest child of Gabriel and Elizabeth Watt.

On December 22, 1824, in Warren County, Kentucky, Lucinda married James Birchfield. Circa 1826 they moved west to the prairies of McLean County, Illinois, where three children were born: Elizabeth, Julia, and Martha.

It is believed that James Birchfield died in the winter of 1835/36. Lucinda married Thomas Huston Wright on August 4, 1836, and from this marriage came four children: John, Elmyra, Silas, and Elijah. In September of 1852 Thomas and Lucinda Wright sold their 171-acre farm to Thomas O. Rutledge, and on March 15, 1853, with their children, some with families of their own, they began the overland journey to Oregon.

Here, on the Sublette Cutoff, Lucinda Birchfield Wright, age 47, died on June 25, 1853. The cause of death is unrecorded. Her nephew, John G. Wright, recalled the burial:

Uncle Huston's wife died on the Green River desert and was buried at the side of the road. I shall never forget how desolate we felt as we hitched up the oxen and pulled out, leaving the freshly broken earth by the side of the Old Oregon Trail as the only visible sign that one of our number had finished the journey, while we must still travel on. There were four families of us that stopped to bury my aunt, in a blanket in a shallow grave, with a few feet of earth and the wide sky over her.

The Wright wagon train arrived at Salem, Oregon, on September 15, 1853. Thomas Huston Wright became a merchant dealing in cattle. On February 21, 1869, he married again to Eliza Stutzman. Nephew John G. Wright became a prominent citizen of Salem where he served two terms as mayor. He was also elected to the Oregon State Legislature as representative from Marion County.

A wooden headboard that is believed to be the original grave marker was found over the Wright grave in 1961. It was removed and is now on display at the Museum of the Mountain Man in Pinedale, Wyoming.

Research and Funding by the

OREGON-CALIFORNIA
TRAILS ASSOCIATION

In Cooperation with the Bureau of Land Management, Green River Resource Area

1998

This is a part of your American heritage. Honor it, protect it, preserve it for your children.

Nancy Jane Hill Grave

Randy Brown

General Comments - A light covering of snow lay on Dempsey Ridge the morning of July 5, 1852, while the Hill family wagons were pulled off to the side of the Sublette Cutoff, as sixty or so family members gathered to lay to rest twenty-year-old Nancy Jane Hill.

One hundred and thirty-six years later, almost to the day, on the bright sunny morning of July 6, 1988, vans, pickups, and 4x4s pulled off to the side of the old Sublette Trail, possibly right where the Hill wagons had corralled. Descendants of the Hill families, OCTA members, and friends—about fifty in all—had gathered to rededicate the Nancy Jane Hill grave.

Speculation and legend surround the woman lying in the grave, but Nancy—that "goddess of a girl"—will continue to have appeal for us just as she had for her legendary "bereaved suitor." The mystique of her grave was summarized by relative Stephen Jackson: "We like to think her grave was so well preserved because she was so well loved."

For more information about Nancy Hill, refer to two articles by Reg Duffin, "Here Lies Nancy Hill?" *Overland Journal* 1, no. 1 (July 1983): 4-13; and "The Nancy Hill Story: The Final Chapter," *Overland Journal* 4, no. 4 (Fall 1986): 56-64.

Location - North of Kemmerer, Lincoln County, Wyoming. Extreme SE corner, Sec. 30, T23N, R117W.

Ownership - Public Land, Bureau of Land Management.

Access - Open to the public.

Directions - From Kemmerer drive north on U.S. 189. At the township of Frontier, veer left on Wyoming 233 and drive north approximately 3.5 miles. Just before Hams Fork bridge, make sharp left turn on a county gravel road. Drive approximately 11 miles northwest to the intersection with the Sublette Cutoff. Drive west to the grave.

NANCY JANE HILL

In April 1852, four brothers, Wesley, Samuel, James, and Steven Hill, together with their families, 62 persons in all, left Paris, Monroe County, Missouri, for California.

There were two deaths along the Platte River and here on the Ham's Fork Plateau Nancy Jane Hill, second eldest of the six children of Wesley and Elizabeth Hill, died of cholera, July 5,1852, age twenty years.

Nancy's uncle, James Hill, wrote: "She was in good health on Sunday evening taken unwell that knight worst in the morning and a corps at nine o'clock at knight".

On the Forty-Mile desert in Nevada Nancy's father, Wesley Hill, died August 24, 1852, and was buried at Ragtown at the Carson River.

The Hill train settled in Soscol Valley, Napa County, California.

Legend has it that Nancy Jane's fiance returned three times over a period of 53 years to tend the grave.

Research by
Stephen Jackson
Stockton, California
(Relative of Nancy Jane Hill)
and the

Funding by
P. Hartwell Gillaspy
Stockton, California
(Great-grand-nephew
of Nancy Jane Hill)

OREGON-CALIFORNIA TRAILS ASSOCIATION

1987

This is a part of your American heritage. Honor it, protect it, preserve it for your children.

Elizabeth Paul

Randy Brown

General Comments - This grave on the Lander Road is located in beautiful Wyoming mountain country. Its unique setting is heightened by the surviving 140-year-old lodgepole pine under which emigrants gathered on July 27, 1862, to bury Elizabeth Paul.

Several of Elizabeth Paul's descendants, including great-granddaughter Frances Nation of Salt Lake City, attended the dedication of the OCTA marker on July 27, 1990, at the gravesite.

Location - Salt River Mountains approximately 30 miles northwest of Big Piney, Lincoln County, Wyoming. SW¼, Sec. 23, T29N, R116W.

Ownership - Public land, Bridger-Teton National Forest, Kemmerer Ranger District.

Access - Open to the public.

Directions - The site is in a remote area of the Bridger-Teton National Forest. Visitors are advised to obtain directions and a map from the Forest Service offices in Afton, Kemmerer, or Big Piney. The recommended route to the grave is from Big Piney, 30 miles west from the edge of town, following the Lander Trail. Several other emigrant graves can be visited en route to the Paul grave.

ELIZABETH PAUL

In April 1862 the Thomas Paul family left Fremont, Iowa, for Washington Territory. Mrs. Elizabeth Mortimore Paul, who was pregnant, had a difficult time on the journey west, and here on July 27, 1862, age 32, she died giving birth to a daughter. The infant, named Elizabeth for her mother, lived for only a week.

The death and burial are well recorded by several contemporary diarists.

Hamilton Scott: "We remained in camp all day. Thomas Paul's wife died about 9 o'clock this morning . . . She has been poorly for some time. We buried her this evening under a large pine tree and put a post and paling fence around her grave."

Jane A. Gould: Monday, July 28, 1862. "Came past a camp of thirty-six wagons who had been camped some time here in the mountains . . . there was a woman died in their train yesterday, she left six children and one of them only two days old, poor little thing it had better died with its mother, they made a good picket fence around the grave."

H. M. Judson: Tuesday, July 29, 1862. "We pass this afternoon a beautiful grave made in an opening in the forest and directly beneath a fine fir tree—Twas made on the 27st inst (only 2 days ago) and was enclosed in a picket yard of hewn timber—a board set into a notch sawed into the tree informed us that the grave contained the remains of Mrs. Elizabeth Paul— aged 32 years—beneath some kind friend had pinned a paper on which were written 3 beautiful & appropriate verses & which I regret very much I had not time to copy."

These verses apparently were written by James S. McClung, a member of the Paul company. In his diary entry for July 27, he notes the death and burial of Elizabeth Paul and then writes the following lines:

Friends and physytions could not save	For tho it was her lot to die	And while she rests beneath this tree
This mortal lovely boddy from the grave	Hear a mong the mountains high	May holy angals wach and see
Nor can the grave contain it here	Yet when gabriels trump shall sound	That naught disturbs her peaceful clay
When God commands it to appear	Among the blessed she will be found	Until the dawning of the day

Julius Merrill: August 15, 1864. "Passed a grave enclosed by a picket fence, painted white. A lovlier spot I never saw. There was an opening of perhaps, half an acre, with one large shady pine near the center. Under this lone tree was the grave. The beauty of the place and the care bestowed upon the remains of the woman caused us all to look at it."

Thomas Paul, with his seven surviving children, continued to Washington Territory and settled in Walla Walla County where he died September 29, 1904, at the age of 75. The original pine tree still stands sentinel here over his wife's grave.

Research, Funding and Signing by the:

OREGON-CALIFORNIA TRAILS ASSOCIATION

In cooperation with the Bridger-Teton National Forest, Kemmerer Ranger District, and descendants of Thomas and Elizabeth Paul

1990

This is a part of your American heritage. Honor it, protect it, preserve it for your children.

IDAHO

The McAuley Cutoff

Randy Brown

General Comments - This marker stands at a highway rest area between two State of Idaho historical markers that interpret "Big Hill" and the McAuley Cutoff. The OCTA marker is a predecessor to the McAuley state sign. For a time the OCTA marker was mounted in the town museum in Montpelier, but in 1993 it was retrieved and installed at its originally-intended location where it now stands. For more on the McAuley marker, see the October 1994 issue of *News From the Plains*.

Location - Southeast of Montpelier, Franklin County, Idaho. SW¼, Sec.16, T14S, R45E.

Directions - From Montpelier drive south on U.S. 30. The rest area is about 10 miles southeast of town, on the east side of the highway.

Access - Open to the public.

Ownership - State of Idaho.

THE McAULEY CUTOFF

On April 7, 1852, 17 year-old Eliza Ann McAuley, with her older brother Thomas and sister Margaret, left Mt. Pleasant, Iowa, to travel overland to California. For a time they were accompanied by the "Eddyville Company" led by William Buck and Ezra Meeker.

Eliza Ann left a notable diary account of the journey west and here on July 15 she wrote:

Traveled ten miles today and camped on Bear River. Just before coming to the river we had the hardest mountain to cross on the whole route. It was very steep and difficult to climb, and we had to double teams going up and at the summit we had to unhitch the teams and let the wagons down over a steep, smooth sliding rock by ropes wound around trees by the side of the road. Some trees are nearly cut through by ropes. The boys fished awhile then took a ramble around the country and discovered a pass, by which the mountain can be avoided by doing a little road building.

On July 17 the Meekers went on toward Oregon, but William Buck remained behind with the McAuleys. Here they stayed for fourteen days building a road around Big Hill.

On July 24 Eliza wrote: "We have 8 or 9 hands today to work on the road. The boys want to get it finished to save people from having to cross that dreadful mountain."

One hired hand, William H. Hampton of Galesburg, Illinois, wrote on July 24: "Still laying over and working we get $2 per day.

Hot and sultry working at the foot of the mountain."

The road was completed by July 29 and the McAuleys continued west leaving Thomas McAuley and William Buck to "remain on the road a week or two to collect Toll and pay the expenses of making it."

On present-day maps the cutoff begins on private ranch land on Sheep Creek about five miles east. From that point Highway 30 follows the approximate route of the cutoff around the south base of Big Hill some seven and a half miles to this point.

On August 7, 1852, John McAllister took the cutoff: "by going it you avoid a long ascent, a long steep & rough & dangerous descent."

On August 13 Cecelia Adams wrote: "the new road is two miles farther but saves some very high mountains."

No references can be found of use of the cutoff in subsequent years. Rising waters of the Bear River may have washed the road away or perhaps nature, unchecked, took control again with a new growth of thickets and brush.

The McAuley or "Eliza Ann" Cutoff will never rank among the great cutoffs of the Oregon-California Trail, but it does reflect the initiative and thought of a group of young Americans in the year 1852.

The McAuleys reached California on September 18. Two years later Eliza Ann married Robert Seeley Egbert. She died in Berkeley, California, November 16, 1919, at the age of eighty-three.

Research, Funding, and Signing by the
OREGON-CALIFORNIA TRAILS ASSOCIATION

1992

This is a part of your American heritage. Honor it, protect it, preserve it for your children.

Shepherd-Wright Massacre

Randy Brown

General Comments - This grave is located along a well-preserved remnant of the Hudspeth Cutoff near Malta, Idaho. The site of the massacre itself can be visited by traveling the Forest Service road approximately 13 miles east. About ¾ mile beyond Sublett Trough the road turns south. The trail continues east into a canyon. The attack site is about ¼ mile down this canyon. The fence around the graves was built by land-owner Lyle Adams who also assisted in the installation of the marker. For more information, see the October 1994 issue of *News From the Plains*; and Randy Brown, "Attack on the Hudspeth Cutoff," *Overland Journal* 12, no. 2, (Summer, 1994): 17-31.

Location - About 18 miles east of Malta, Cassia County, Idaho. NE¼, Sec.9, T13S, R29E.

Directions - Take Exit 245, Sublett Road, off I-84. Go east on Sublett Road. In 2.5 miles veer right. The graves are about 6 miles farther across a fence on the right side of the road. Ask locally for the Lyle Adams ranch. The ranch-house is about 2 miles west of the graves.

Access - Permission is required to visit the site.

Ownership
Lyle Adams
HC 61 Box 1116
Malta, Idaho 83342
(208) 645-2238

SHEPHERD-WRIGHT MASSACRE

On July 27, 1859, a wagon train consisting of twenty men, women, and children, was attacked by Shoshone Indians in a canyon on the Hudspeth Cutoff, thirteen miles east of here. Four men were killed. This is the probable site of their grave.

The Shepherd-Wright company of Fayette, Missouri, was en route to California when it arrived at the Twin Springs campground about twenty miles east of here on the evening of July 26, 1859. The company was captained by Thomas Furgeson Shepherd, of Ione City, California, who was accompanied by his two brothers, William and James, and their families. Traveling with them were James D. Wright, his wife and their three children. Several hired men were also in the company.

Indians had been harassing the emigrants at Twin Springs, and on the morning of July 27 Captain Shepherd was advised to remain in camp. He ignored the warnings and ordered his company forward. They were attacked after they had traveled seven miles into a deep canyon, and Captain Shepherd, William Shepherd, Claiborne Raines, and William Diggs were killed. The Wright family, three of whom were badly wounded, was left at the wagons, while the other survivors fled back to Twin Springs.

On July 28 several combined companies moved forward to the attack site, rescued the Wrights and gathered the dead. Late that afternoon they camped near here on Sublett Creek and buried the four men.

Mrs. William Shepherd wrote: *"My husband and his brother Furgeson were laid side by side, and Claiborne Raines and William Diggs, the four; were buried in one grave. A wagon body sheltered them from the cold earth."*

Emigrant Henry Pomeroy wrote: *"At dusk this evening a wide grave was dug by the roadside & the four bodies consigned to it in silence & sadness. The lamentations of Mrs. [William] Shepherd over her dead husband was heartrending & touching. A headstone was placed at the grave with the facts of the affair & the names of the deceased on it."*

The gravesite was preserved by landowner Wes Adams in whose family the story of the grave had been handed down since earliest settlement times. Although names and exact dates had been forgotten, this grave was traditionally known as the final resting place of "four men who were killed by Indians," now identified as Diggs, Raines, and the two Shepherd brothers who died July 27, 1859.

Researched and Placed by the

OREGON-CALIFORNIA TRAILS ASSOCIATION
1994

This is a part of your American heritage. Honor it, protect it, preserve it for your children.

Raft River

Emil Kopak photo circa 1930, used in identification of gravesite.

Nebraska State Historical Society

Reg Duffin (left) and Randy Brown at the gravesite.

Dorothy Duffin

General Comments - In 1991 Randy Brown returned rocks covering three graves to their original location, and landowner Lyle Woodbury granted permission to place this marker. Woodbury constructed the fence around the graves, and he and his wife Carol continue to care for the site. Lyle and Carol Woodbury received OCTA's "Friend of the Trail" award in 1993. Recognition is also due to pioneer Oregon Trail researcher Emil Kopak of Oshkosh, Nebraska, whose photograph of the graves taken ca. 1930 made the identification and subsequent restoration of the site possible. For more information see the April 1994 issue of *News From the Plains.*

Location - Raft River, Cassia County, Idaho. NW¼, Sec. 7, T10S, R28E.

Directions - Take Exit 15 from I-86 to the community of Raft River. It is about 50 miles west of Pocatello and about 12 miles east of Burley. Inquire locally for the Woodbury farm. It is about 3 miles south of the interstate.

Access -Permission to visit the site is required.

Ownership
Lyle and Carol Woodbury
Starr Route, Box 54
Declo, Idaho 83323

RAFT RIVER

On or about September 20, 1843, a California-bound emigrant party consisting of twenty-five people and six wagons approached the Oregon Trail crossing of the Raft River. Before they reached the river, however, they turned south and established what became the main route of the California Trail to the Humboldt River, via the Raft River Valley and Goose Creek. They were led by mountain man Joseph Reddeford Walker, who had taken the route in reverse when he returned from California in 1834.

In 1844 the route was used by the Stephens party, which apparently was guided through this area by Isaac Hitchcock, former fur trapper. On September 13, 1844, James Clyman, who was en route to Oregon, wrote:

> *Last night contrary to our expectations we came to a brook with a broad valley of fine grass this brook is called cassia [Raft River] & is the place whare Mr. Hitchcock left our rout & went South with 13 wagons in company for California.*

Eventually this place, west of the Oregon Trail crossing of the Raft River, became the established point of departure from that trail for California emigrants, as well as for a few parties who took the southern route into Oregon. The use of this junction was partially superseded in 1849 and in later years by the establishment of the Hudspeth and Salt Lake cutoffs. This "parting-of-the-ways," however, was never entirely abandoned and in fact enjoyed a rebirth of popularity when the Lander Trail was opened in 1859.

On August 1,1850, Byron McKinstry wrote:

> *The Oregon Road takes up the bluff and follows the course of the [Snake] River while we keep to the left and follow the creek [Raft River] nearly to its source. I notice some fishing this morning and with some success. Crossing the creek we followed up the bottom, the creek on our left for 5 or 6 m., the bottoms narrow, the bluffs low but rocky and almost perpendicular.*

Graves were noted at this place by several passing emigrants. In 1849 J. Goldsborough Bruff wrote, "... we reach'd Raft River, forded it, and just over, on our right, a grave. (Just where the Oregon trail turns off right, over basaltic cliffs.)—"To the Memory of Lydia Edmonson who died Aug.15. 1847, Aged 25 years.'"

On August 11,1862, J. S. McClung noted the death of Elizabeth Adams, age twenty-six, of Marion County, Iowa. She had been mortally wounded during the incident at Massacre Rocks. On August 12 he wrote: "she was buried near Raft river—by the side of G W Sanders from Kekuk Iowa who died hear July 27th 1862 aged 33 year near here I noticed the grave of Mifs[?] Hays who died 1852. [Possibly Henry Hays of Indiana, who died in August 1852 near the Raft River] at this place the road forked the left hand leading to calafornia"

While the identity of these graves may never be known with certainty, they may indeed be those of Edmonson, Sanders, Hays, or Elizabeth Adams. Whoever they are, the American pioneers buried here deserve to be remembered, and their final resting place commemorated and preserved for all time.

Researched and Placed by the
OREGON-CALIFORNIA TRAILS ASSOCIATION
1992

This is a part of your American heritage. Honor it, protect it, preserve it for your children.

The Stricker Store

Virginia Ricketts

General Comments - The Stricker Store and homesite, also known as the Rock Creek store and stage station, consists of an 1865 log store and an early twentieth-century, two-story frame house. A small cemetery that includes the graves of two emigrant children, a freighter, a murder victim, a horse thief, a gypsy woman, and an early local resident is situated just west of the store. The site and buildings are listed in the National Register of Historic Places. See Ralph W. Macy, "Stricker's Store," *Overland Journal* 4, no. 2 (Summer 1986): 25-35.

Location - About 8 miles southeast of Twin Falls, Twin Falls County, Idaho. NE¼, Sec. 22, T11S, R18E.

Ownership
Idaho State Historical Society
210 Main St.
Boise, ID 83702

Site Admistration
The site is administered by:
Friends of Stricker Ranch, Inc.
P.O. Box 2218
Twin Falls, ID 83303

Access - The site is open to the public, but permission is required to tour the house. A caretaker lives in a portion of the house and is willing to provide tours of the house and site if contacted in advance. The caretaker is Tom Lloyd, 3715 Stricker Cabin Road, Hansen, ID 83334, (208) 423-4000.

Directions - Take the Hansen Exit from I-84. Go 5 miles south of Hansen and 1 mile west.

STRICKER STORE
ROCK CREEK, IDAHO

The waters of Rock Creek and the grass that grew along its banks provided a welcome oasis for travelers traversing the arid Snake River Plain. This combination caused the area to become a favorite camping site for Oregon Trail emigrants and a crossroads during the development of nineteenth century roads.

In 1864, Ben Holladay chose this site for a home station on his Overland Stage Line.

The U.S. Army established Camp Reed near here in 1865 to protect travelers, and James Bascom built the Rock Creek Store. The store soon became a popular stopping place for emigrants, freighters, miners, and cowboys. On August 31,1888, Sarah Hall Pulliam noted, "this Rock Creek Store is a great blessing to the emigrants. . . . So as they can get a Sack of flour for their selves, and something to feed their starving teams on. . . ."

In 1876 Herman Stricker purchased the store and remained the proprietor until it closed in 1897. One of the cellars behind the store served as the first jail for the area. In 1878 Chief Buffalo Horn and his followers camped in the vicinity only days before the start of the Bannock Indian War. Stricker and his wife, Lucy, built the house just east of the store in 1890. It replaced one destroyed by fire the previous year. A small cemetery nearby contains the graves of three emigrants.

Research, signing, and funding by the:

OREGON-CALIFORNIA
TRAILS ASSOCIATION

May 1989

This is a part of your American heritage. Honor it, protect it, preserve it for your children.

Randy Brown

Gravesite two miles west of Soda Springs, Idaho.

Emil Kopak, Wyoming State Archives

Unidentified grave at Glenns Ferry, Idaho, now believed lost.

OREGON

Oregon Trail: Blue Mountain Crossing

Dick Ackerman

General Comments - Using donations given to the Maurice Burchfield Memorial Fund, the Northwest Chapter of OCTA marked the Blue Mountain Crossing of the Oregon Trail on National Trails Day, June 3, 1995. A permanent monument consisting of a bronze plaque mounted on a granite rock was developed and installed thanks to the efforts of longtime personal friends of Maurice Burchfield, Dick Ackerman, and Lowell Tiller. "Burch" put in a lot of time locating and marking the trail remnants across the Blues. He was a loyal, dedicated OCTA member and a good friend to all who knew him.

Location - Approximately 20 miles northwest of La Grande, Umatilla County, Oregon. SW¼, Sec. 31, T1S, R36E.

Directions - Eighteen miles north of La Grande, take the Mt. Emily Exit from I-84 (Exit 243) and drive east about ¼ mile to a small parking area on the south side of the road. The monument is at the back or south edge of the parking area, adjacent to one of two swales of the trail coming from the south.

Access - Permission is required to visit the site.

Ownership -
Pendleton Ranches, Inc.
Cunningham Sheep Company
303 SE Third St.
Pendleton, OR 97801

OREGON TRAIL BLUE MOUNTAIN CROSSING

NORTHWEST CHAPTER
OREGON-CALIFORNIA
TRAILS ASSOCIATION

M. ("BURCH") BURCHFIELD
MEMORIAL
1995

David R. Koontz

Emil Kopak photo of the David R. Koontz grave, circa 1930.

Nebraska State Historical Society

Lowell Tiller

General Comments - Biographical information on David Koontz and family was provided by Mildred Koontz of Abany, Oregon. OCTA past president Dick Ackerman and OCTA director Lowell Tiller built the fence around the grave.

The city of Echo donated equipment and the cost of manpower to improve access and parking at the grave site. For more on the Koontz grave, see the April 1995 issue of *News From the Plains*.

DAVID R. KOONTZ

David R. Koontz was born in Gallia County, Ohio, in 1839, and was buried here in 1852. He was the fourth child and youngest son of Martin V. Koontz, bridge builder and carpenter, and Lydia Richabough. The Koontz family was originally from Virginia. From there they moved to Ohio and in 1841 to Wapello County, Iowa. The urge to move farther west came in 1852, and the Koontz clan took the trail to Oregon. F. M. Koontz later wrote, "When we came to Oregon it was like a tribal migration. There were 24 wagons in our train, all members of the train being related."

Family reminiscences indicate the train was raided by Indians while along the Platte River, resulting in the loss of seven horses. This meant a long walk to Oregon for some who had originally planned to ride.

While passing Names Hill on the Sublette Cutoff near present-day La Barge, Wyoming, D. R. Koontz carved his name and the date July 7, 1852, on the north face of the bluff along with five other members of the party, all from Wapello County.

There is no record of how David died. The only other family death recorded was that of David's brother-in-law, Moses Hale, who died from cholera. Hale also left his name inscribed on Names Hill.

Oregon-bound emigrant James S. McClung passed this grave on September 27, 1862. Like Koontz, McClung was from Wapello County:

> traveled several miles & passed the grave of Mr. David Coontz from Dahlonega Wappelo county Iowa   he was buried about 4 rods on the right hand side on the side of a small hill   the grave was covered with poles which were quite rotten   the head bord was rotted off at the ground but still lying by the grave   the letters were cut with a knife & were plane & distinct   near here the road crossed the river whare we camped after travellng 15 ms

Boy Scouts found the grave in 1915, built a fence around it, and erected a headstone. The city of Echo has been instrumental in the restoration of the site and in placing this marker.

Researched and signed by

OREGON-CALIFORNIA TRAILS ASSOCIATION

1993

This is a part of your American heritage. Honor it, protect it, preserve it for your children.

Location - Outside Echo, Umatilla County, Oregon. SW¼, Sec.15, T3N, R29E.

Directions - From the center of Echo, drive east and cross railroad tracks. Turn right on old U.S. 30. The grave is about ¼ mile south, on the west side of the road.

Access - Open to the public.

Ownership - State of Oregon.

Butter Creek Crossing

Lowell Tiller at the Butter Creek Crossing marker.

Dick Ackerman

General Comments - Because of the abundance of good water and grass in an otherwise arid location, Butter Creek was a favored emigrant camping spot. It also became a burial area. Among those buried there was Lucinda Powell Propst. In later years, all her remains that were found were moved to the cemetery in Echo, Oregon.

Since the trail era, Butter Creek has been changed by the Army Corps of Engineers and agricultural development until it barely resembles the stream it used to be.

Location - Southwest of Hermiston, Umatilla County, Oregon. SW¼, Sec. 20, T3N, R28E.

Ownership - The State of Oregon.

Access - Open to the public.

Directions - Exit I-84 south of Hermiston, Oregon, on Oregon 207 and travel south 5 miles. The marker is at a pull-off on the west side of the road, where the Oregon Trail intersects the highway.

BUTTER CREEK CROSSING
THE OREGON TRAIL

The Oregon Trail came from the east across Echo Meadows and turned southwest just west of here. The Butter Creek crossing of the trail is about one mile to the southwest. Because of the availability of water and grass in the area, it became a favorite campsite where stock were rested and recruited. It was also used as a burial location for emigrants who died.

One of those was Lucinda Powell Propst, who was born in Champaign County, Ohio, on February 19, 1817. In March 1852, with her husband Anthony and their five children, she left Sugar Grove, Illinois, for Oregon. While crossing the Blue Mountains in August, Lucinda became ill and died. Her body was carried in the wagon to the Butter Creek campground for burial. Shortly after leaving there, Anthony Propst became ill, died, and was buried at the Philip Foster place on the western slope of the Cascade Mountains. The five children were taken in by relatives and the wagons proceeded to the Willamette Valley.

Researched and Placed by the: 1990

OREGON-CALIFORNIA
TRAILS ASSOCIATION

This is a part of your American heritage. Honor it, protect it, preserve it for your children.

Catherine Bonnett Butts Grave

Dick Ackerman

General Comments - Forty-four descendants from points as diverse as Alaska, Oregon, California, and Washington, and ranging in age from two to ninety-one, attended the dedication of the marker at the Catherine Bonnett Butts grave on June 4, 1988.

Robert P. Head, who owns the land on which Catherine Bonnett Butts is buried, welcomed preservation efforts at the Butts grave but has a landowner's natural caution about permitting entry on his land. A practical arrangement has been worked out whereby OCTA members may obtain permission to visit the gravesite by producing a current OCTA membership card.

Location - East of Tygh Valley, in Sherman County, Oregon. SE¼, Sec. 28, Rl4E, T3S.

Ownership
Robert P. Head
Box 77 Platterhill Road
Greenville, NY 12083

Access - Permission is required to visit the site.

Ben Ward
58133 Conroy Road
Tygh Valley, OR 97063
(541) 483-2476

Directions - Use Exit 87 off I-84 two miles east of The Dalles, Oregon, to reach U.S. 197. Drive south from the interstate on 197 about 32 miles to Oregon 216 at Tygh Valley. Turn left (east) on Oregon 216 and drive approximately 4 miles and turn left on Conroy Road, shortly after passing a sign for White River State Park. Drive north for a half mile to a locked gate and farmhouse. This is the home of Mr. and Mrs. Ben Ward from whom permission to visit the gave must be obtained. They have the key to the lock on the gate. Drive about 2 miles from the gate to abandoned farm buildings on the right. From there walk past the farm house across the field to the southeast about a half-mile, through a fence, to the gravesite.

CATHERINE BONNETT BUTTS

This is the grave of Catherine Bonnett Butts, who died here on October 2, 1845. She was on the Meek Cutoff Route of the Oregon Trail, descending Hollenbeck Hill to the Deschutes River. This quote is from the diary of a family friend, Samuel Parker:

"October 5... Heare we beried
Missis Butts and 3 More"

There are other graves in the immediate vicinity, all unidentified.

Mrs. Butts was born in 1812 on Little Skin Creek, Weston, Virginia.

Signing by

**OREGON-CALIFORNIA
TRAILS ASSOCIATION**

Research and Funding by

MR. & MRS. L. ROBERT TEMPLEMAN
PALISADE, NEBRASKA

1987

This is a part of your American heritage. Honor it, protect it, preserve it for your children.

Sarah King Chambers

Dick Ackerman

General Comments - Sarah Chambers' grave is located in remote Oregon desert country on the infamous "Meek Cutoff," near the banks of the North Fork of the Malheur River. It is marked by the original headstone. The current fence around the grave was built by Lowell Tiller, OCTA director and coauthor of *Terrible Trail: the Meek Cutoff, 1845* (1966, 1993), and OCTA past-president Dick Ackerman. Visitors to the site should also ask locally for directions to the nearby pioneer cemetery where Oregon trailblazer Levi Scott is buried.

Location - About 25 miles north of Juntura, Malheur County, Oregon.

Directions - Juntura is about 65 miles west of Vale on U.S. 20. From Juntura follow a winding dirt road that leads to Beulah Reservoir. In 22 miles, cross a bridge near an intersection with the road to Westfall. Turn left at the intersection. The grave site is about 2 miles down this road, just off the road to the right, on a small knoll. Look for the log fence. A large hay barn is opposite.

Access - Open to the public.

Ownership - Unknown.

SARAH KING CHAMBERS

Sarah King Chambers was born July 25,1823, in Madison County, Ohio, to Nahum and Serepta King.

In the spring of 1845, she, along with her husband, Rowland, and their children Margaret and James, joined other members of the King family on their migration west. Their destination was the Willamette Valley of Oregon, for a new beginning in a land which held great promise.

With about 1,000 other emigrants and 200 wagons, the King party chose to follow Stephen Meek in an ill-fated attempt to cross central Oregon on their way to the upper Willamette Valley, near present-day Eugene. Meek convinced them that this new route would avoid many hazards of the Blue Mountains, the restless Cayuse Indians, and the perilous journey down the Columbia River.

Their group became known as the "Lost Wagon Train of 1845." Not really lost, but desperate for water in these high deserts, they abandoned their plans for a new route and turned north toward the Columbia River and the established trail to Oregon. They arrived at the mission in The Dalles in October in a most deplorable condition.

Sarah could not complete that journey. She died on September 3,1845, and was buried here, alongside the "Terrible Trail." The cause of death was not recorded in contemporary accounts.

There were twenty-three other known deaths along the cutoff route from where they left the Oregon Trail at the crossing of the Malheur River (in present-day Vale, Oregon) until they rejoined the Oregon Trail at the mission at The Dalles.

Research, Funding, and Signing by the
OREGON-CALIFORNIA TRAILS ASSOCIATION
1991

 This is a part of your American heritage. Honor it, protect it, preserve it for your children.

The Applegate Trail #1

THE APPLEGATE TRAIL

The Applegate Trail crossed the present boundary of Oregon approximately three miles southeast of here and went around the northern end of the lake which covered much of the basin, passing close to where you are now standing. The route was opened in 1846 by a group of trailblazers from the northern part of the Willamette Valley, including Jesse and Lindsay Applegate, Levi Scott, and others, and was first used by pioneers coming from the States in the fall of that year. It was developed as an alternate way to reach the western valleys of Oregon while avoiding the perils of the Columbia River route.

A portion of the trail was used in the fall of 1848 by Peter H. Burnett, who led a group of more than 150 men and fifty heavily loaded wagons from the area of Oregon City, Oregon, to the goldfields of California. They left the Applegate Trail about eight miles south of here and established a new route into the Sacramento Valley. This was the first wheel route connecting the western valleys of Oregon and California.

In 1852 pioneers from the East opened a route off the Applegate Trail from the southern end of Lower Klamath Lake to the Yreka area of northern California.

Research and Signing by the:

**OREGON-CALIFORNIA
TRAILS ASSOCIATION**

1991

This is a part of your American heritage. Honor it, protect it, preserve it for your children.

Location - Malin, Klamath County, Oregon.

Directions - This marker is located next to the main parking area of Malin City Park.

Access - Open to the public.

Ownership - City of Malin, Oregon.

The Applegate Trail #2

THE APPLEGATE TRAIL

In the spring of 1846 pioneers settling in the western valleys of Oregon encouraged the opening of an alternate wagon route from the states to their settlements—one that avoided the perils of the Columbia River, and one free of control by England's Hudson's Bay Company. Jesse and Lindsay Applegate, who both lost sons to the Columbia River in 1843, were among the volunteers for this task. Ultimately the group grew to fifteen, including Levi Scott, John Scott, Moses ("Black") Harris, John Boygus, John Owen, John Jones, Robert Smith, Samuel Goodhew, Bennett Osborn, William Sportsman, William Parker, Benjamin Burch, and David Goff. Jesse Applegate became the leader of the group.

They traveled south from the northern part of the Willamette Valley and passed this area about a mile to the east. Approximately ten miles southeast of here they turned east to cross the Cascade Mountains. They continued east and southeast until they intersected the Fort Hall wagon road to California. The new trail was first used by pioneers coming from the states in the fall of that year.

In 1848 Peter H. Burnett led a group of more than 150 men and fifty heavily loaded wagons from Oregon City to the goldfields of California. He took this route as far as the east side of Tule Lake, then headed south and west, ultimately entering the Sacramento Valley near present-day Chico. This established the first wagon road between Oregon and the Sacramento Valley.

Researched and Placed by the

OREGON-CALIFORNIA TRAILS ASSOCIATION

1993

This is a part of your American heritage. Honor it, protect it, preserve it for your children.

Location - Ashland, Jackson County, Oregon.

Directions - This marker is located in Railroad Park on Main Street in Ashland.

Access - Open to the public.

Ownership - City of Ashland, Oregon.

The Applegate Trail #3

Dick Ackerman

Location - Roseburg, Douglas County, Oregon.

Directions - This marker is located next to the sidewalk on the west side of the Douglas County Courthouse.

Access - Open to the public.

Ownership - City of Roseburg, Oregon.

THE APPLEGATE TRAIL

The Applegate Trail, sometimes referred to as the Southern Road, passed this location in a north-south direction along the route of present-day Main Street. Just north of here the trail turned westerly and crossed the north fork of the Umpqua River near its confluence with the south fork.

The trail was opened in 1846 by a group from the northern part of the Willamette Valley, including Jesse and Lindsay Applegate, Levi Scott, and twelve others. It was intended to serve as an alternate way of reaching the western valleys of the Oregon Territory from the States, while avoiding the perils of the Columbia River route. In addition to bringing settlers to the Willamette Valley, it also helped the settlement of the southwest valleys—many pioneers stopped along the way. The Applegate Trail remained in use until well into the 1860s.

This portion of the trail was used in the fall of 1848 by Peter H. Burnett, who led more than 150 men and fifty heavily loaded wagons from Oregon City to the goldfields of California. They were followed about ten days later by a smaller group from north of the Columbia River. This trip established the first wheel route connecting the western valleys of Oregon and California and remained in use for this purpose for several years.

Researched and placed by

OREGON-CALIFORNIA TRAILS ASSOCIATION

1992

This is a part of your American heritage. Honor it, protect it, preserve it for your children.

The Applegate Trail #4

THE APPLEGATE TRAIL

In the spring of 1846 pioneers settling in Oregon encouraged the opening of an alternate trail from the states to the northwest valleys which would avoid the perils of the Columbia River and a route which was not controlled by England's Hudson's Bay Company. Jesse and Lindsay Applegate, who both lost sons to drowning while coming down the Columbia River in 1843, were two of the first to volunteer for the job.

On the morning of June 20, 1846, a group of trail blazers gathered on the banks of La Creole Creek, today called Rickreall Creek, approximately where you are now standing, to pursue this task. The group ultimately grew to a party of fifteen, each with his own saddle horse, pack horse and supplies, including his own firearms. Jesse Applegate was elected leader of the group, which included Lindsay Applegate, Levi Scott, John Scott, Moses (Black) Harris, John Boygus, John Owen, John Jones, Robert Smith, Samuel Goodhue, Bennett Osborn, William Sportsman, William Parker, Benjamin Burch, and David Goff.

They proceeded south to a point near the California border, then east to a point near the California border, then turned east and southeast to the Humboldt River. The first emigrants to use the new route came over the trail in the fall of that year. It became known as the Applegate Trail, or, as the trailblazers referred to it, the Southern Route.

Researched and Placed by the

OREGON-CALIFORNIA TRAILS ASSOCIATION

1993

This is a part of your American heritage. Honor it, protect it, preserve it for your children.

Location - Dallas, Polk County, Oregon.

Directions - This marker is located on the north side of Rickreall Creek in the Dallas City Park.

Access - Open to the public.

Ownership - City of Dallas, Oregon.

UTAH

Grantsville Markers

Al Mulder

General Comments - These two markers are located on the grounds of the Donner-Reed Museum in Grantsville, Utah, on the route of the Hastings Cutoff-California Trail. The marker project was begun in April 1996 and completed August 9, 1996. The project was initiated by the Utah Crossroads Chapter of OCTA and jointly sponsored by the Tooele County Historical Society. The project was funded with corporate donations and individual contributions from members of Utah Crossroads. The Tooele County Commission was a major contributor. Grants were received from the Utah Pioneer Sesquicentennial Council and the Utah State Historical Society. Utah Crossroads volunteers planned and coordinated the project and installed the panels. Al Mulder of the Crossroads Chapter was project manager. The Tooele County

Historical Society collected the aragonite stone used in the pedestal and arranged for the masonry work.

On August 11, 1996, the 150th anniversary of the death of John Hargrave, these markers were dedicated.

Location - Grantsville, Tooele County, Nevada. NW¼, Sec. 36, T2S, R6W.

Access - Open to the public.

Directions - Proceed west on U.S. 40 through Grantsville, turn north on Cooley for one block to the corner of Cooley and Clark. The museum is located at the southwest corner of the intersection, on the west side of the street.

Panel of Grantsville Marker

Emigrant Graves . . .

Utah's First Emigrant Graves

In August 1846, the first emigrants to take the Hastings Cutoff to California arrived in the Tooele Valley. They left two of their number behind. John Hargrave, traveling with the Harlan-Young Party, died of pneumonia on August 22 and was buried the next day. The Donner-Reed Party reached the valley two weeks later. On August 26, a member of their company, Luke Halloran, died of consumption and was buried "at the side of an emigrant who had died in the advance company." Historians have suggested present-day Granstville or Lake Point as the site of these graves. Though the exact location may never be known, this panel commemorates John Hargrave and Luke Halloran, the first emigrants buried in Utah Soil.

Panel of Grantsville Marker

Twenty Wells

Emigrants bound for California in 1846 rested in this vicinity because of the cold, pure, spring water welling up from holes in the ground. These holes were six inches to nine feet in diameter and more than 70 feet deep. When water was dipped

out it was replaced immediately from an underground source but did not overflow the hard sides. Because of this phenomenon the springs were called wells. Twenty of these wells were scattered over the area of present-day Grantsville.

Some of the first emigrants called the area Hastings Wells, named for Lansford W. Hastings, who pioneered a wagon route to the Humboldt River near Elko, Nevada. This alternate route to the California Trail through Tooele Valley was used by emigrants and gold-seekers from 1846 through 1850. The plentiful grass and water in the valley made it a major campsite and resting place for wagon trains and pack parties taking the Hastings Cutoff.

Donner Spring Historic Site

Al Mulder

General Comments - The Donner Spring historic marker consists of a three-panel wood kiosk, sheltering three fiberglass embedment interpretive panels: Donner Spring, Salt Desert Trail, and Pilot Peak. The spring pond and kiosk are enclosed by a wood three-rail and post fence and access gate.

The fencing project began in 1993, and the fencing and kiosk were completed in June 1994. The site was dedicated August 14 as part of the 1994 OCTA convention at Salt Lake City. The project was sponsored by the Utah Crossroads Chapter and funded with private contributions from members of OCTA and a donation by the Utah Westerners Foundation. The fencing and kiosk construction was done by Utah Crossroads volunteers. The project manager was Vern Gorzitze.

Location - On the T L Bar Ranch, approximately 21.5 miles north of I-80 Exit 4. The exit is a few miles east of Wendover, Box Elder County, Utah. NE¼, Sec.36, T4N, R19W.

Directions - I-80 Exit 4 is about 115 miles west of Salt Lake City. There is a truck stop on the north side of the freeway at this exit. The T L Bar Ranch and Donner Spring is 21.5 miles north on the gravel road that leaves the interstate at this point. The road is rough, dusty, or muddy and should be driven only when dry, and then preferably in a pickup or utility vehicle.

Access - Permission to visit the site is required.

Ownership
TL Bar Ranch
Dean R. Stephens

Panels at Donner Spring Historic Site

Pilot Peak

Pilot Peak rises 10,716 feet (3,266 meters) from the southern sprawl of the Pilot Range, beckoning desperate travelers crossing the tortuous Great Salt Desert of the Hastings Cutoff. Like Chimney Rock on the Great Plains, this landmark in the desert guided countless souls during the 1840s and '50s to its haven of precious water, grass and wood on its eastern slopes. Capt. John C. Frémont, who crossed its 90 miles of waterless expanse in October, 1845, wrote his scouts: Kit Carson, Auguste Archambault, Lucien Maxwell and Basil Lajeunesse ". . . had found at the peak water and grass, and wood abundant. The rearing up was quick done and in the afternoon we reached the foot of the mountain, where a cheerful little stream broke out and lost itself in the valley. The animals were quickly turned loose, there being no risk of their straying from the grass and water. To the Friendly mountain I gave the name of Pilot Peak. . . . Some time afterward, when our crossing of the desert became known, an emigrant caravan was taken by this route, when then became known as The Hastings Cutoff."

"On the opposite side of this valley rose abruptly and to a high elevation another mountain (Pilot Peak), at the foot of which we expected to find the spring of fresh water that was to quench our thirst, and revive and sustain the drooping energies of our faithful beasts."
Edwin Bryant 1846

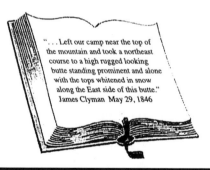

". . . Left our camp near the top of the mountain and took a northeast course to a high rugged looking butte standing prominent and alone with the tops whitened in snow along the East side of this butte."
James Clyman May 29, 1846

SALT DESERT TRAIL

The faint trail coming over the ridge to the east and extending westward through the sage and across the salt plain to Donner Spring was first travelled by Kit Carson, Auguste Archambault and two others as they scouted in advance of Captain John C. Frémont's company of topographical engineers on their way to California in late October 1845. Lansford W. Hastings with James Clyman and James Hudspeth came east over the trail in May 1846 as they explored the route that became known as the Hastings Cutoff. Later that summer Hastings and Hudspeth led several hundred people west over this trail. These included the Bryant-Russell mounted party, the Harlan-Young wagon train, the Hoppe Party together with Heinrich Lienhard and others including T. H. Jefferson. The Donner-Reed company brought up the rear after abandoning several wagons on the salt flats. Later, argonauts by the hundreds crossed this way during the summer of 1850. Although mostly abandoned by California emigrants after that time in favor of the better route north of Great Salt Lake, the Hastings Road for many years provided access to local ranches and mines.

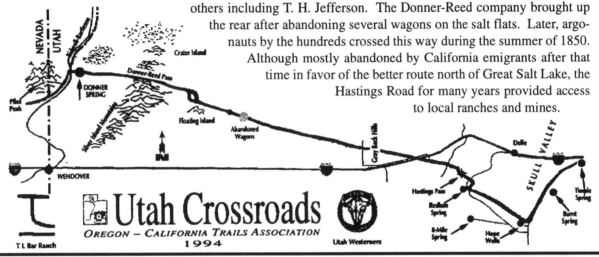

DONNER SPRING

The Bidwell-Bartleson party of 1841 made the first recorded visit to the springs along the eastern base of Pilot Peak as they moved south along the edge of the Salt Desert on their way to California.

Donner Spring was rediscovered in October 1845 by Captain Frémont's guides, Kit Carson and others. When retracing Frémont's trail eastward in late May 1846, James Clyman and Lansford W. Hastings "encamped on a fine spring Brook."

By early July 1846, Lansford Hastings had succeeded in persuading several emigrating parties to take his untried Cutoff around the south shore of Great Salt Lake. By mid-August, guided by Hastings, the large Harlan-Young wagon train reached the spring after a difficult crossing of the Salt Desert. Heinrich Lienhard, traveling close behind, described the spring as a fine one about 4 by 6 feet across and from 4 to 5 feet deep, the water fresh and good.

T.H. Jefferson, the map maker of the 1846 emigration, marked eleven springs in the area and named them "Bowark Wells."

The Donner-Reed party reached the spring two weeks later in early September after suffering severe hardships from lack of water on the eighty-three mile Salt Desert crossing.

NEVADA

Bidwell Pass Marker

General Comments - The Bidwell Pass historic marker kiosk is located on public land and was installed in the summer of 1998. A thirty year right-of-way permit allowing OCTA to place the marker was granted to the Utah Crossroads Chapter of OCTA by the Bureau of Land Management through the Elko Field Office in February 1998. The marker is a large interpretive panel mounted on a steel "easel" type frame and sheltered by a wooden kiosk.

The Bidwell Pass marker project began in fall 1997 after the Long Distance Trails Office, National Park Service, gave approval to use Donner Spring Cost-Share Project #5 funds for a related California Trail marker. The project is sponsored by the Utah Crossroads Chapter and was funded by NPS Cost-Share funds. Labor to construct and install the kiosk and to prepare the site was donated by Utah Crossroads volunteers.

Location - Approximately 13 driving miles north of I-80 Exit 4. This exit is a few miles east of Wendover, Utah. The marker is in Elko County, Nevada. NW¼ SE¼, Sec. 17, T31N, R70E.

Directions - See directions for the Donner Spring marker. The Bidwell Pass marker is about 13 miles north of the freeway on the road heading north from Exit 4.

Access - Open to the public.

Ownership - Public lands administered by the Bureau of Land Management.

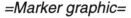
=Marker graphic=

=Marker graphic=

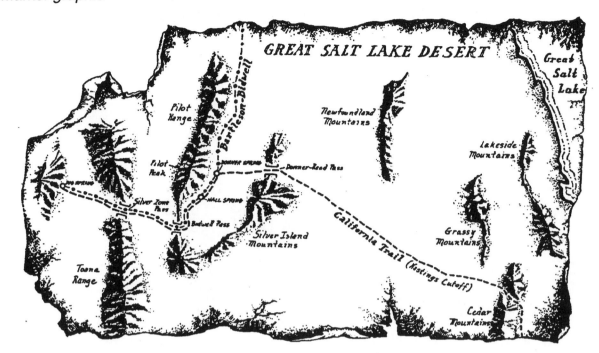

=Marker text and diary quotes=

Over Bidwell Pass to the Humboldt

Before you is Bidwell Pass, named for the Bidwell-Bartleson party, the first emigrant company to journey overland to California. In August and September of 1841, this group of 32 men and an 18-year-old mother with her baby daughter, left the Oregon Trail at Soda Springs, Idaho, and crossed Utah north and west of the Great Salt Lake. At Big Spring, in eastern Nevada, they abandoned their remaining seven wagons and pressed on to California.

In the summer of 1846, the Bryant-Russell pack party and the Harlan-Young, Hoppe-Lienhard, and Donner-Reed wagon companies followed the Hastings Cutoff around the south side of the lake. The two trails merged before crossing Bidwell Pass. Ensuing years saw other California emigrants and gold-seekers travel the cutoff. The route, however, was no shorter than the established trails from Fort Hall or Soda Springs to the Humboldt River. In fact, because of the long drive without water or feed for animals crossing the Great Salt Lake Desert, it was more difficult. The route was abandoned after 1850 in favor of the safer Hensley Salt Lake Cutoff, north of the Great Salt Lake.

"Passed a number of good springs. Took dinner at one of them [Halls Spring]. We traveled on the border of the salt plain until night. . . . These plains border on the salt lake. In the evening we left the salt plain, turned our course to the west, crossed the mountain through a gap [Bidwell Pass] and could find no water."
—James John, September 14, 1841

"After traveling about ten miles we struck a wagon-trail, which evidently had been made several years before. From the indentations of the wheels, where the earth was soft, five or six wagons had passed here. . . . Following this old trail some two or three miles, we left it on the right and crossed some low and totally barren hills. . . ."
—Edwin Bryant, August 5, 1846

Humboldt Highlands Historic Site

Dedication ceremony, 1996. Paul Sawyer at the podium.

Bob Pearce

General Comments - This marker and kiosk were built to commemorate the sesquicentennial of the Donner Party and the Hastings Cutoff. It is located opposite the confluence of the main Humboldt River with the South Fork of the Humboldt. California emigrants of 1846 who traveled the Hastings Cutoff emerged from the South Fork's canyon to rejoin the main route of the California Trail. Most of them did not reach this point until September.

The marker was sponsored by Elko members of the California-Nevada Chapter of OCTA and was financed by corporate and private donors. The crew that built the kiosk and installed the marker consisted of Bud Gibson, Charles Greenhaw, Jack Griswold, Dick Immenschuh, Bob Pearce, Harry Peterson, Paul Sawyer, and Mel Steninger.

The marker was dedicated on August 18, 1996, during the OCTA convention held at Elko, Nevada.

Location - About 9 miles west of Elko, Nevada.

Directions - Drive west from Elko on I-80 to Exit 292. The marker is on the north side of the freeway adjacent to a small parking area.

Access - Open to the public.

Ownership - State of Nevada. (Right-of-way, Interstate 80.)

Road to California

Europeans had lived in the New World 300 years before they made trails along the Humboldt River. Peter Skene Ogden and his British fur brigade were the first to meet the native Shoshone. The trappers passed this site going east in 1828. In 1833, an American fur party led by Joseph Walker trapped in the area.

The first California emigrants to cross Nevada, the 1841 Bidwell-Bartleson group, had nearly exhausted themselves before they found the Humboldt; their wagons were abandoned 80 miles east of here. The first ruts here were cut in 1843, when Joseph Walker veered from the Oregon Trail to the Humboldt with three wagons.

Still to come beyond this point were the obstacle of Palisade Canyon; the crossing at Gravelly Ford near the original site of the Maiden's Grave; the marshy approach to Stony Point near Battle Mountain; the difficult passage through sandy hills near Golconda, where the Donner Party's J. F. Reed killed John Snyder.

In one of history's great human migrations, entire families of settlers, gold seekers, felons and saints passed here, mostly headed for the new Eden and gold.

The peak year was 1852. In 1869, the Central Pacific Railroad linked East and West and people could cross Nevada at 15 miles an hour instead of 15 miles per day.

Fateful Hastings Cutoff

Overland emigrants of the 1840s were ever searching for shortcuts to the West Coast. Crude maps and bad judgment mixed with personal ambition created the notorious Hastings Cutoff, which reconnected with the California Trail two miles southwest of this site.

Lansford Hastings had never seen the route that bears his name when he suggested a "more direct way" from Ft. Bridger to California in his emigrants' guide of 1844.

Capt. John Fremont's 1845 expedition crossed the Salt Flats of Utah and explored passes of the Ruby Mountains, those great barriers to wagons. In the 1845–46 winter at Sutter's Fort, Hastings heard of Fremont's route, but he did not travel the great loop around the Rubies. Hastings met emigrants in Wyoming and persuaded several groups, the Donner Party the last of them, to take an unproved wagon road.

Most travelers survived the trials of the cutoff: Deep canyons and thickets in the Wasatch, an 80-mile waterless stretch of salt flats, and the grand circuit deep into Nevada. The route cost the Donner Party three weeks, making it a starvation wagon train.

The Gold Rush revived the route in its final years, 1849 and 1850. The gold-seekers, many of them destitute and begging, rejoined the California Trail near this site.

The Humboldt River

In the valley overlooked by this monument flows the Humboldt River. Emigrants joined it 50 miles to the east at Humboldt Wells. It meanders a distance of 375 miles from headwaters in Elko County to its termination in an alkali sink, the fate of all Great Basin rivers.

A chronicler, Dale Morgan, calls it the Highroad of the West. He also describes it as "that turgid, green, barren-banked and sullen river."

This was the last discovered of the American rivers. First named for Peter Skene Ogden, trapper and explorer; it was then called Mary's River after Ogden's Indian wife; also the Barren River, for its lack of trees; and then placed on maps as the Humboldt, namesake of Baron Alexander von Humboldt.

The Humboldt traces an east-west arc through Nevada's north-south-oriented mountain ranges and its river plain was the route for emigrants heading to California. Its maligned waters, alkaline, brackish, and sometimes non-existent, sustained grasses that allowed travelers' animals to survive the desert journey.

Its sink, near present-day Lovelock, marked the beginning of yet another perilous leg of the emigrants' journey, the 40-mile Desert.

Gravelly Ford
Unknown Emigrant Graves

Randy Brown

General Comments - Nearly one hundred members of the California-Nevada Chapter of OCTA helped fence and mark the unknown emigrant graves at Gravelly Ford, Nevada, on Memorial Day weekend 1989. After they finished the work at Gravelly Ford, they went on to install the marker at the Susan Coon grave at Antelope Springs on the Applegate-Lassen Trail.

Location - Approximately 6 miles east of Beowawe, Eureka County, Nevada. SW¼, Sec. 1, T31N, R49E.

Ownership
Zeda, Inc.
Horseshoe Ranch
Beowawe, NV 89821
(702) 468-0421

Access - Permission is required to visit site.

Directions - Exit I-80 at Exit 145, Beowawe-Crescent Valley. Proceed south 4.5 miles to Horseshoe Ranch complex on right of highway and ask for permission to visit the site.

From the ranch complex, return 1 mile north toward I-80 and turn right onto a dirt ranch road. Be sure to close the gate behind you (leave all gates closed or open, as you find them). Proceed 1 mile to a point at which the road branches—take the right branch. Proceed 0.7 mile to a second branch—take the left branch. Proceed 0.6 mile to a third branch—take the right branch. Proceed 0.5 mile to the site. The historic Gravelly Ford of the Humboldt River is directly below the gravesites.

GRAVELLY FORD
UNKNOWN EMIGRANT GRAVES

"They are buried in shallow graves, the earth heaped above them, and a stake bearing the single word 'unknown' placed at the head."
—John Steele Diary, 1850

Of the many thousands of graves of emigrants who died and were buried along the overland trails, only a very few can still be located and associated with a specific name. Some of the names of the dead were not known to their companions, as John Steele recounts above. Most were known to their fellow travelers and were named, but the names and sites were soon lost to the elements.

There are several unknown emigrant graves in this vicinity. At one time, it was thought that one of these graves might be that of John Snyder of the Donner Party, killed in 1846 by James Reed in one of the most famous overland trail incidents. Historians now agree that this notorious event took place considerably farther west along the Humboldt River at or near Iron Point, a few miles east of Golconda.

Just below this grave site is the famous Gravelly Ford, where the emigrants traveling westward down the Humboldt River crossed over to the south side for the first time. From this point all the way to the Humboldt Sink, a distance of several hundred miles, trails followed both sides of the river.

A famous emigrant grave, the so-called "Maiden's Grave," is located across the river and several miles farther to the west at the Beowawe Cemetery. This is the grave of Lucinda Duncan, a grandmother who died in 1863. Her grave was first noted by the crews building the Central Pacific Railroad, and was carefully tended by them over the years. In 1906 realignment of the railroad caused the grave to be moved to the cemetery, where it is marked by a large white wooden cross.

Research, Signing and Funding by the

OREGON-CALIFORNIA
TRAILS ASSOCIATION

May 1989

This is a part of your American heritage. Honor it, protect it, preserve it for your children.

Lucinda Parker Duncan

Bob Pearce

General Comments - Lucinda Duncan's husband Daniel Duncan accompanied Elijah P. Howell to California in 1849. This Howell-Duncan company was captained by Judge Daniel Parker of Ray County, Missouri, who was Lucinda Parker Duncan's cousin and brother-in-law. Elijah P. Howell's diary was published by OCTA as Number 1 of the Emigrant Trails Historical Studies Series. See Susan Badger Doyle and Donald E. Buck, eds., *The 1849 California Trail Diaries of Elijah Preston Howell* (Independence, Mo.: Oregon-California Trails Association, 1995).

Randy Brown, assisted by Elko OCTA members Bob Pearce, Tony Primeaux, and Dick Kazanis, placed the marker in June 1997. A dedication ceremony organized by Bob Pearce and two of Lucinda Duncan's descendants, Bev Cannon of Lakeview, Oregon, and Carolyn Stewart of Kingman, Arizona, was held later that summer. Many Duncan family descendants attended. For an article on Lucinda Duncan, see Carolyn Stewart, "Journey West, 1863: The Wagon Train of Lucinda Duncan," *Overland Journal* 15, no. 2

(Spring 1997): 24-30. Visitors to the site should also see nearby Gravelly Ford of the Humboldt River (see the entry for the OCTA Gravelly Ford marker).

Location - About 3 miles east of Beowawe, Eureka County, Nevada.

Directions - From I-80 take the Beowawe Exit to Wyoming 306 and drive south 5.8 miles to the railroad tracks, just beyond the Humboldt River. From the tracks, bear left (southeast) through the town for 0.4 miles. Turn left on a gravel road. The cemetery is 2.2 miles east at the top of a bluff. Look for the large white cross that marks the Duncan grave.

Access - Open to the public.

Ownership
Eureka County
The cemetery is maintained by the
Crescent Valley Historical Society
Crescent Valley, NV 89821

LUCINDA PARKER DUNCAN

The grave of Lucinda Duncan, called "The Maiden's Grave," reportedly was moved a short distance to its present site during realignment of the Southern Pacific Railroad in 1906. Far from being a maiden, Lucinda Duncan was a seventy-one-year old grandmother traveling with her family to Galena, Nevada, from their home near Richmond, Ray County, Missouri in 1863.

The daughter of John and Charlotte Parker, Lucinda was born in Fauquier County,Virginia, ca. 1792. Early in life she moved with her parents to Anderson County, Kentucky, where she married Daniel Duncan on December 11, 1820. Around 1830 Daniel and Lucinda moved with their first four children to Ray County. Four more children were added to the family in Missouri. In 1849 Daniel and his three oldest sons joined a wagon train captained by Lucinda's cousin, Judge Daniel Parker. Daniel Duncan died in the California gold fields late in 1849. Lucinda Duncan remained a widow for the rest of her life.

In 1863 Lucinda and her family decided to emigrate to Nevada, then in the middle of a gold and silver mining boom. Lucinda was called "the mother of the wagon train" as it consisted primarily of her seven surviving children, their wives and husbands, many grandchildren and various other close relatives. Lucinda, still strong and vigorous at the age of seventy, occasionally drove her own horse-drawn carriage, the only team of horses in the company of sixty ox teams and wagons.

Family stories say that she suffered a heart attack on the trail above Gravelly Ford, lingered for a day, and then died the night of August 15. The only contemporary account comes from the diary of James Yager, one of the contingent of non-Duncans in the train.

Sunday Morning 16. An event occurred last night that has cast a gloom over our camp; the death of one of its members. An old lady the mother and grandmother of a large part of our train. She had been sick for several days & night before last she became very ill so much so our train was compelled to layover yesterday & last night she died. She was pious and beloved by the whole train, relatives & strangers. Her relatives took her death very hard. All of her children and grandchildren were present except a grandson who is in the confederate army.

Camp Wide Meadows Monday 17. We left Camp Reality yesterday about noon. Before leaving Mrs. Duncans funeral was preached by Captain Peterson. [Peterson was captain of another train.] Her remains were carried to its last resting place as we proceeded on our journey & up on a high point to our left about one mile from camp, we paid our last debt & respect to the   remains of the departed mother. There upon that wild & lonely spot, we left her, until Gabriel shall sound his trumpet in the last day. The scene was truly a sad one to leave a beloved mother on the wild & desolate plains. A board with the name of the desceased was put up at the head & boulders was laid over the grave to keep wolves from scratching in it. After this the train moved on.

Signing and funding by **The Oregon-California Trails Association**

1997

This is a part of your American heritage. Honor it, protect it, preserve it for your children.

Susan Coon

Randy Brown

General Comments - The Susan Coon grave is located near the beginning of the Applegate Trail. Years ago, vandals broke the original headstone that had been placed on the grave, and half of the stone is now lost.

Antelope Springs, which gave the emigrants the last water until they reached Rabbithole Springs some 17 miles ahead, is up the draw beyond the Susan Coon grave.

For a driving guide to this segment of the Applegate Trail, see Devere Helfrich, Helen Helfrich, and Thomas Hunt, *Emigrant Trails West: A Guide to Trail Markers Placed by Trails West, Inc. ...* (Reno, Nev.: Trails West, Inc., 1984).

Location - Approximately 20 miles west of Imlay, Pershing County, Nevada. SW¼SE¼, Sec. 28, T33N, R31E.

Ownership - Public land, Bureau of Land Management.

Access - Open to the public.

Directions - A high clearance vehicle is recommended. Exit I-80 at Exit 145, the Imlay Exit. Pass under the freeway toward Imlay and go west 1 mile on the frontage road. Turn north onto the Imlay-Sulfur gravel road. Proceed 6 miles and cross the Humboldt River on the Callahan Bridge. You are now in Lassen's Meadow, where emigrants camped and recruited their animals. Proceed 13.7 miles farther on the gravel road to a branch—take the left branch. Proceed 1.5 miles and turn left onto a very rough two-track road. Continue slowly on the rough road for 1.3 miles to a small turnaround. Antelope Springs is directly ahead, in the ravine. The Susan Coon grave is up the hill to the left of the turn-around area, in a clump of small trees and bushes.

SUSAN COON GRAVE

Susan (Susannah) McCord Coon, wife of Isaac Coon, died from the complications of child-birth at this site on August 11, 1860, while on the way to California from Coles County, Illinois. The child, Robert E. Coon, born on August 9, survived and was taken on to California by his father, with the aid of other members of the party.

Frank Dunn, a stonecutter traveling with the wagon train, spent the night carving the original headstone from native rock. An additional grave marker has been subsequently placed by Susan's descendants.

This is one of the very few emigrant graves along the overland trails with its original headstone.

Research, Signing and Fencing by the: **OREGON-CALIFORNIA TRAILS ASSOCIATION**

May 1989

This is a part of your American heritage. Honor it, protect it, preserve it for your children.

The Carson River
40-Mile Desert Route

Chuck Dodd

General Comments - The marker is placed at the edge of fine swales of the emigrant trail left in the sand. As you stand facing the marker, raise your arms out away from your body and you will be pointing in the direction the emigrants traveled. You can easily walk into the large swales to the right.

Location - Just northwest of Fallon, Churchill County, Nevada. SW corner, almost on southern line, Sec. 32, T20N, R28E.

Ownership - Public land, Bureau of Land Management.

Access- Open to the public.

Directions - Leave U.S. 50 at the west edge of Fallon, Nevada, turning north onto Soda Lake Road. At the intersection there is a prominent sign reading "Coast Guard Station, Soda Lake." Proceed 4.3 miles on Soda Lake Road and turn left onto an unmarked dirt road. Passage may be very difficult in wet weather. Proceed 0.8 mile west. The marker is to the right of the road, near a large tree.

On the way back to U.S. 50, consider taking Workman Road 0.7 mile to the rim of Soda Lake. From Soda Lake Road, the small extinct volcano that holds Soda Lake appears to be a low hill. You can drive up onto the rim and look down into the lake.

THE CARSON RIVER
40-MILE DESERT ROUTE

"I frequently counted thirty or forty carcasses at one encampment, and in one place 100 wagons in less than a mile, all in sight at once - many of them in good order, others split into pieces or partially burned. Everything that constitutes a Cal. outfit except grubb lies along the road in profusion; clothing, tents, harness, tools, &c., water casks innumerable that have been brought all the way for this desert are now thrown away"   —Byron McKinstry, 1850

This section of the historic California Trail was opened from the Sink of the Humboldt River to the Carson River at Ragtown in the fall of 1848 by a wagon train of emigrants captained by Joseph B. Chiles. From Ragtown, the trail followed the Carson River westward to a junction with the Carson Pass trail.

This forty-mile dry crossing was one of the most dreaded and most chronicled ordeals of the entire overland emigrant experience. Coming as it did so near the end of the overland journey —when supplies were low, stock were weak, and wagons in poor condition—it was a great challenge to the courage and fortitude of the emigrants.

One of the wonders along the trail, often referred to and often visited by the emigrants, was Soda Lake, two miles southwest of this site:

". . . by the Spring on the desert, there is a large lake of Salt water, it is almost Strong enough for brine to save meat with, this is another of the curiosities found on a California trip—"   —Leander V. Loomis, 1850

Over the years, more emigrants were to travel this particular route to California than any other route.

Research and Signing by the:

OREGON-CALIFORNIA TRAILS ASSOCIATION

Funding Donated by:

The Ormat Group

In Cooperation with the United States Bureau of Land Management, Carson City District

State and federal laws protect historic and prehistoric artifacts on public land.
This is a part of your American heritage. Honor it, protect it, preserve it for your children.

Lassen-Clapper Murder Site

General Comments - In 1990, one hundred and thirty-one years after the killing of Peter Lassen and Edward Clapper in the Black Rock Desert in Nevada, a rock hound found some human bones exposed at the mouth of a canyon on the western side of the Black Rock Range. This chance discovery, first treated as a possible recent homicide by the Nevada authorities, set in motion a series of forensic investigations by the F.B.I. and the Smithsonian Institution in Washington, D.C., which determined that the remains were almost certainly those of Edward Clapper. With the concurrence of Clapper's descendants, OCTA, and the Lassen County Historical Society, with the cooperation of the Winnemucca District of the BLM and the Masonic Order, returned Clapper's remains to California to be interred adjacent to Peter Lassen's burial site in Honey Lake Valley, just south of Susanville. OCTA and the Nevada BLM then erected this marker at the site where the Clapper remains were discovered, so that the actual historical location of the double killing would not be lost again due to the passage of time.

Tom Hunt

Location - In the Black Rock Desert northwest of Winnemucca, Humboldt County, Nevada. NE¼, Sec. 7, T38N, R26E.

Ownership - Public land, Bureau of Land Management.

Access- Open to the public.

Directions - Just west of the small community of Gerlach, Nevada, at the "Y" intersection, take the right paved road to Soldier Meadows (the left fork is the continuation of Nevada 447 to Vya). The road to the site from this point is along the western edge of Black Rock Desert playa and the eastern base of the Granite Range. Drive

about 13 miles, then turn right (north) onto a graded gravel road to Soldier Meadows and Summit Lake. Drive approximately 40 miles to Mud Meadows Reservoir Dam. Upon crossing the dam, immediately turn right (south) on a bladed road along the eastern flank of the Black Rock Range. Drive 8.3 miles, turn left (east) on unmarked Clapper Creek Road, and drive 1.4 miles to a "T" intersection. Turn right (south) and drive 0.7 mile to the murder site and marker at the mouth of a canyon. Inquire at Gerlach about road conditions. If conditions permit, time may be saved by turning to the right (east) on the Wheeler Reservoir road off the Soldier Meadows-Summit Lake road approximately 44 miles from Gerlach itself (or approximately 30

THE PETER LASSEN AND EDWARD CLAPPER MURDER SITE

The renowned pioneer, Peter Lassen, first passed this spot in 1848 while guiding a small party of American emigrants to his rancho in California. They were following the Applegate Trail, also known as the Southern Route to Oregon, which passed through the Black Rock Desert approximately three miles to the west. This important trail was opened into the Willamette Valley in 1846 by a party of explorers from Oregon led by Jesse and Lindsay Applegate and Levi Scott. On his 1848 trip, Lassen left the trail at the southern end of Goose Lake in northeastern California and opened the Lassen Trail into California. It is estimated that half of the 1849 overland gold seekers to California followed this combined Applegate-Lassen route.

On April 26, 1859, Peter Lassen and Edward Clapper were slain at this site while on a prospecting trip. The men were camped by the large boulder to the right when shots rang out from the rocky cliffs above. A third companion, Lemericus Wyatt, managed to escape and ride bareback without sleep or food to the settlements in Honey Lake Valley.

The remains of both Lassen and Clapper were buried here by a party from Honey Lake Valley shortly after the murders. Peter Lassen's remains were retrieved by a party of Free Masons in November of 1859 and reburied near Susanville beneath a monument commemorating his achievements. Although the public decried the fact that Clapper's remains were left at the site, no one ever returned to retrieve them. Over time the location of the site was lost. In May, 1990, recreationists discovered Clapper's remains eroding out of the stream bed adjacent to the large boulder. Clapper was reburied adjacent to the Lassen Monument in 1992. Several theories about the murder have been proposed, but the identity and motive of the assailant(s) remain a mystery.

Research and text provided by the
Bureau of Land Management
and the
Oregon-California Trails Association.

Marker placed by the
OREGON-CALIFORNIA TRAILS ASSOCIATION
1995

This is a part of your American heritage. Honor it, protect it, preserve it for your children.

miles from the turnoff onto Soldier Meadow-Summit Lake road). This shorter route is often impassable at the ford of Mud Meadows Creek, but it comes into the previously described driving route just opposite Clapper Creek Road, and saves the long northward detour to Mud Meadows Reservoir Dam. Always use extreme caution when driving in this very remote area. Use four-wheel drive vehicles only on these routes.

Lloyd Dean Shook - died 1854.   Lassen Trail, California.

CALIFORNIA

The Alford-Cameron Gravesite
Bruff's Camp

Beverly Hesse photos

*OCTA improved the site and
installed a marker in 1994.*

*The site in 1991 before OCTA improved
it and installed a marker.*

General Comments - Bruff's Camp is located on the rugged and remote divide between Deer and Mill Creeks northeast of Chico, California. The condition of the roads is highly variable from year to year depending on the weather and timber operations. Extreme care should be exercised when entering this area, and it is wise to consult local Forest Service offices as to road and driving conditions. Don't attempt to reach the site without four-wheel drive.

Location - About 30 miles northeast of Chico, Tehama County, California. NE¼, Sec 30, T27N, R3E.

Directions - The site can be reached from the east via active logging roads by turning north from California 32 onto the main logging road along the crest of the Deer Creek/Mill Creek Divide at a point 1 mile west of the junction of California 32 with California 36/89. This route closely approximates the route of the original Lassen Trail, but because of the opening and closing of branch logging roads on a yearly basis, driving directions are almost impossible to give. The best plan would be to travel this route with someone familiar with it. Barring that, one should simply stay on the main road along the divide and always keep bearing to the west. Bruff's Camp is located 0.9 mile west of the Narrows (marked) and 0.7 mile west of the intersection with Ponderosa Way.

From the north, turn south off California 36 at Paynes Creek and drive approximately 20 miles southeast on Ponderosa Way to the dead-end junction with the previously described road along the top of the Deer Creek/Mill Creek Divide. Turn right and drive 0.7 mile to Bruff's Camp, located south of the road. In the above distance the road drops down into Mill Creek Canyon and climbs back up to the crest road along the divide.

The site may be accessed from Cohasset, which is approximately 15 miles north of Chico. From Cohasset it is about 20 miles to Bruff's Camp. Drive north from Cohasset to Deer Creek. Continue to the top of the Deer Creek/Mill Creek divide ridge. The road will turn to the east on the ridge. As described above, the gravesite is 0.7 miles west of the intersection with Ponderosa Way. If the site is missed while heading east on the ridge, return 0.7 miles from the intersection with Ponderosa Way to locate Bruff's Camp.

THE ALFORD-CAMERON GRAVESITE BRUFF'S CAMP

In a common grave at this site—or in close proximity to it—are buried four emigrants who were killed by a falling tree while on their way to California via the Lassen Trail in 1849. Three of the men were members of the Alford family—the father and two sons; the other was a young friend of one of the sons. Thanks to the detailed account kept by J. Goldsborough Bruff, the man for whom this campsite is named, we know the full story of this tragic event.

A large oak tree, rotted at its base, crashed down upon the four men during a rainstorm as they slept in a tent below. None died instantly; all died agonized deaths within a few hours. The following is a portion of Bruff's account of the burial and the exact words which he inscribed upon the headboard of the common grave.:

". . . We laid down pine slabs at first, in bottom of the grave; and now cut a hole at the foot, and a gro[o]ve at the head, centrally, and put in a stout ridge pole, about 18 ins: above the breasts of the bodies. The wagon-cover was thrown in over the dead, pine slabs laid along, from the sides to the ridge pole, the ends up, so as to form a roof, and we then filled in and smoothed over the grave.

"I procured the tail-board of a wagon, and scratched and painted together the following inscription, and put it up.

Ormond Alford, aged 54 yrs.
and his sons.—
William M., aged 19,
and Lorenzo D. aged 15 years
And John W. Cameron, aged 22 yrs.
The 3 first of Kendall Co. Ill.:
formerly of Peru, Clinton Co. N.Y.
and the last, of Will Co. Ill:
Killed by the falling of an oak tree
upon them, while asleep in their
tent, near this spot, about
1 A.M. Oct. 31st. 1849.
Epitaph.—
Their journey is ended, their toils are all past,
Together they slept, in this false world, their last;
They here sleep together, in one grave entombed,—
Side by side, as they slept, on the night they were doom'd!"

Research, Signing and Funding by:

OREGON-CALIFORNIA TRAILS ASSOCIATION

In Cooperation with Roseburg Resources Company

1991

This is a part of your American heritage. Honor it, protect it, preserve it for your children.

The final approach to the site is from California 32 by way of Forest Service Road 27NO8. This road branches north from California 32 approximately 6 miles northeast of Soda Springs and drops down to cross Deer Creek before climbing to the top of the divide to join the crest road coming west from Deer Creek Meadows. Drive west along the divide on the combined route via the Narrows to the Ponderosa Way junction and continue 0.7 mile west to the site. Do not attempt any of these approaches during wet conditions. This is strictly a dry season outing.

Access - Open to the public.

Ownership - Public lands administered by the Forest Service.

Sonora: Emigrant Trail Terminus

Tom Hunt

Location - Intersection of Greenley and Mono Streets, Sonora, California.

Directions - From Highway 49 (Washington Street) going south in Sonora, turn east (left) on Mono Street and proceed to Greenley. From Highway 106 (Sonora Pass Highway) take Old Wards Ferry Road north to the Mono/Greenley intersection.

Access - Open to the public.

Ownership - City of Sonora, California.

SONORA: EMIGRANT TRAIL TERMINUS

Sonora was the goal of many emigrants traveling the various overland and sea routes.

The 1852 Clark-Skidmore Party of emigrants from Elizabethtown, Ohio, and Lawrenceburg, Indiana, struggled to forge a wagon trail up the Walker River and over the 10,000-foot pass east of Sonora. In 1852, more than 2,000 emigrants with 20,000 cattle followed, creating a new emigrant road to Sonora.

Difficult for wagon travel, the Walker River and Sonora wagon route was soon abandoned. The Emigrant Wilderness Area in the high country has been named to honor these pioneers. Following major changes, the trail became an important passenger and supply route between the Bodie gold regions and Sonora.

Dedicated by the
Oregon-California Trails Association
and the
E Clampus vitus, Matuca Chapter
February 18, 1996

Grove C. Cook

Tom Hunt

General Comments - According to Nicholas "Cheyenne" Dawson, Grove Cook joined the Bidwell-Bartleson Company sometime after they had started and "begged to be allowed to pay his way by driving our wagon, as he could furnish nothing."

By all accounts Cook was one of the more colorful characters of early California. He often told the story of the "conflict" between the American and Mexican forces during the Battle of Santa Clara, January 2, 1847, when the two armed battalions, camped about one mile apart, traveled all day to reach each other but did not succeed. California historian Clyde Arbuckle often quoted Cook as having said of the incident, "They fit like hell all day to keep from gettin' within two miles of each other."

Evidently Cook had a temper and once killed an Indian during a dispute over a wild horse. Hubert H. Bancroft summed up Cook by writing: "He is described as a man whose wit and generosity went far to counterbalance some less desirable qualities."

Location - Evergreen Cemetery, Santa Cruz County, California.

Directions - Evergreen Cemetery is located at the west side of Harvey West Municipal Park in Santa Cruz. Take the River Street off-ramp from California 1 and proceed 1 block north on River Street. Turn left on Coral Street. Drive west and south to the end of Coral Street and then turn right on Evergreen Street. The cemetery is located on the left along the base of the hill; Harvey West Park is to the right. The Cook marker is located in plain view, toward the center of the cemetery, above the main walkway.

Access - Open to the public.

Ownership - City of Santa Cruz, California.

GRAVE OF GROVE C. COOK

Grove C. Cook, a native of Kentucky, came to California in 1841 as a member of the Bidwell-Bartleson Party, the first overland emigrant wagon train to set out from the United States to cross the continent to the Pacific Slope.

The party was forced to abandon its wagons in eastern Nevada after blazing a trail across the desert immediately north of Great Salt Lake. The party, after detouring south along the eastern flank of the Sierra Nevada in order to find a crossing, entered Mexican Alta California by way of Walker Pass and the Kern River at the southern end of the San Joaquin Valley. They arrived at Dr. John Marsh's ranch at the base of Mt. Diablo in Contra Costa County on November 4, 1841, after an arduous journey of nearly six months.

Cook worked for John C. Sutter at Sutter's Fort in Sacramento for several years before settling in the Santa Clara Valley. He took part in the war with Mexico and in California's bid for statehood. He served on the alcalde's committee for the Pueblo de San Jose, operated a boarding house for a time, and was active in political affairs in California's early years.

In 1845 he bought the Rancho de los Capitancillos near San Jose on which the New Almaden quicksilver mine was later developed. He thus became the first American to own a part of his historic mine. In recognition of this association, a piece of cinnabar ore, donated by the New Almaden Quicksilver County Park Association, is affixed to the base of this monument.

His first wife, Sophronia, sister of the Sublette brothers of fur trapping fame, divorced him while he was en route to California in 1841. At Sutter's Fort on December 28, 1845, he married Rebecca Kelsey, who had come overland to Oregon in 1843, and then to California the following year.

Several other early-day emigrants are also buried in Evergreen Cemetery. Among them are: William Blackburn, member of the Swasey-Todd Party of 1845, members of the Imus family of the Joseph Aram Party of 1845; and members of the Arcane family who braved Death Valley in 1849.

Cook died on February 15, 1852, while on a visit to Santa Cruz.

In cooperation with the Santa Cruz Historical Trust, this marker has been placed by the California-Nevada-Hawaii Chapter of the Oregon-California Trails Association to commemorate the 150th anniversary of the Bidwell-Bartleson Party

OREGON-CALIFORNIA
TRAILS ASSOCIATION

September 28, 1991

This is a part of your American heritage. Honor it, protect it, preserve it for your children.

Nancy Kelsey

Randy Brown

General Comments - The grave of Nancy Kelsey is located on the rim of Cottonwood Canyon in the foothills of the Sierra Madre Mountains in southern California, about midway between Bakersfield and Santa Maria. The marker was placed at the grave on Thanksgiving weekend 1994. A dedication ceremony was held by the California-Nevada Chaper of OCTA on April 1, 1995. For more on the Kelsey grave see the April 1995 issue of *News From the Plains*.

Location - Approximately 50 miles east of Santa Maria, Santa Barbara County, California.

Directions - In Cuyama or New Cuyama ask for the ranch of Bonnie Goller. The ranch is about 15 miles west of New Cuyama, a few miles south of Highway 166.

Access - Permission is required to visit the site.

Ownership
Bonnie Goller
P.O. Box 206
New Cuyama, CA 93254
680-7220 (cellular)

NANCY KELSEY

Nancy Kelsey, the first American woman to reach California by the overland route, was a member of the Bidwell-Bartleson Party of 1841. This party reached the San Joaquin valley ranch of John Marsh on November 4 after having crossed the summit of the Sierra Nevada near present Sonora Pass.

Nancy Roberts Kelsey was born August 1, 1823, in Barren County, Kentucky. With her family she soon moved to Jackson County, Missouri, where at age fifteen she married Benjamin Kelsey. Their first child, Martha Ann, was born about December 15, 1839.

The Kelseys joined the party of sixty-four emigrants who rendezvoused in early May 1841 at Sapling Grove, eight miles outside Weston, the fur company outfitting town on the Missouri frontier. These prospective emigrants intended to take "Sublette's Trace" to the Rocky Mountains and then find their way to California.

After an uneventful crossing of the plains, while camped on August 11 near Soda Springs in present Idaho, the company split. Thirty-four of the original party, including Benjamin, Nancy, and Martha Ann, turned south for California. On September 11, while in present northwest Utah, the Kelseys were forced to abandon their wagons. From then on, for nearly three months, Nancy rode horseback or walked, carrying her child across deserts and mountains until the end of the journey. One of her companions, Nicholas ("Cheyenne") Dawson, later wrote his recollection of her as they traveled down the rugged western slope of the Sierras:

"Once, I remember, when I was struggling along trying to keep Monte [his horse] from going over, I looked back and saw Mrs. Kelsey a little way behind me, with her child in her arms, barefooted I think, and leading her horse—a sight I shall never forget."

The Kelseys had ten children in all and over the years lived in various places in California and Oregon, earning and losing several small fortunes. While at Sonoma in 1846 the Kelseys were involved in Fremont's "Bear Flag Revolt." Nancy is sometimes called the Betsy Ross of California for her part (with several other women) in sewing together the original California Bear Flag.

Benjamin Kelsey died in Los Angeles in 1889. Nancy left the city and homesteaded about 2.5 miles west of here in Kelsey Canyon where with her family's help she built a small cabin. During the last year of her life she suffered from an incurable cancer, and when near death Nancy asked that she be buried in a real coffin, "not something scraped up with old boards." Nancy Kelsey died August 10, 1896, while staying at the home of her daughter, Nancy Rose Clanton, which was located not far from the gravesite. She is buried between two children who died in 1895, a granddaughter and one other, now known only as "Baby Plummer."

By all accounts Nancy Kelsey must have lived her life as she was described by Joseph B. Chiles, a traveling companion of her youth, who, many years later, wrote of her as he knew her on the trail in 1841: *"She bore the fatigue of the journey with so much heroism, patience and kindness that there still exists a warmth in every heart for the mother and her child, that were always forming silver linings for every dark cloud that assailed them."*

Signing and Funding by **OREGON-CALIFORNIA TRAILS ASSOCIATION**

1994

Appendix

Additional known graves, not marked by OCTA.

Bean grave, outside Guernsey, Wyoming.

Ephraim Brown,
Rock Creek, Wyoming.
See Randy Brown, "The
Death of Ephraim Brown,"
Overland Journal 7, *no. 1*
(1989): 26–28.

J.H., 1861.
Probably a footstone.
Horse Creek, Wyoming.
Five miles east of
Independence Rock.

*Lucinda Rollins, from Dayton, Ohio,
died June 15, 1849. Guernsey, Wyoming.*

Wyoming State Archives

Emil Kopak, Wyoming State Archives

*Jo Barnette - died August 26, 1844. Stone inscribed by Jim Clyman.
Mrs. Bryan - died July 1845. South side of Sweetwater River, at the Ninth Crossing.*

Emil Kopak, Nebraska State Historical Society

Sarah Thomas - died June 29, 1854.
Seminoe Cutoff, Wyoming. Circa 1930.

Wyoming State Archives

Malinda Armstrong - died August 15, 1852.
Cherokee Trail, Currant Creek, Wyoming.
Forty miles south of Rock Springs.

Charlotte Dansie,
Pacific Creek, Wyoming.

Randy Brown

Wyoming State Archives

George B. Platt of Canton, Ohio - died 1849. Deer Creek, Wyoming. Grave and stone moved to Glenrock Cemetery.

George B. Platt stone today in Glenrock cemetery. This stone is a copy of the original which was broken. Platt was listed as the captain of his company and was buried near the east bank of Deer Creek.

Randy Brown

Joel Leabo - died June 11, 1849. Cassa, Wyoming.

Wyoming State Archives

Index